Hindustani Music Today

To

My mother,
Smt. Kamlini Raja

Who gave me my love of music and
of literature besides so much else

Hindustani Music Today

Deepak Raja

With a Foreward by
Arvind N. Parikh

PRINTWORLD
Publishers of Indian Traditions

Cataloging in Publication Data — DK

[Courtesy: D.K. Agencies (P) Ltd. <docinfo@dkagencies.com>]

Raja, Deepak.

    Hindustani music today / Deepak Raja.

      p.   cm.

    ISBN 13: 9788124606162

    1. Hindustani music — History and criticism.   I. Title.

DDC 780.954   23

Published and printed by:

D.K. Printworld (P) Ltd.

Regd. Office: '*Vedaśrī*', F-395, Sudarshan Park

(Metro Station: Ramesh Nagar)

New Delhi – 110 015

Phones: (011) 2545 3975; 2546 6019; *Fax:* (011) 2546 5926

E-mail: indology@dkprintworld.com

Website: www.dkprintworld.com

Foreword

Deepak Raja is, indeed, a "Deepak" — a brilliant light — of our Gharana.

As a musicologist, with profound and realistic insights into the intricate world of music, he has to his credit several thought-provoking books. As a sitar and surbahar player, he displays the style of our Gharana with authenticity and sincere capability.

This book, titled Hindustani Music Today will be of immense value to both, the initiated as well as readers with average knowledge. Deepak Bhai has truly succeeded in delving into various dimensions of art music with great insight, projecting the same through easy-to-understand language, and enabling the reader to absorb various facets of music. He has abstained from making any authoritative conclusions leaving the reader to naturally grasp the basics of our music.

The book comprises various chapters, judicially structured to follow a systematized sequence, going from the fundamentals to the final conditions through performance.

I feel happy to write this short foreword for a valuable book authored by a worthy student, and wish it all the success it deserves.

Mumbai, 15 August 2011 **Arvind N. Parikh**

Preface

This book attempts to present a panoramic view of Hindustani art music as viewed at the dawn of the 21st century. It addresses educated readers, who may not have been introduced to Hindustani music in their early years, but have been drawn to it as mature adults. The objective is to share with them an intelligent perspective on what this music is, where it comes from, and where it might possibly be going. Resulting from this perspective, the reader may feel better equipped for future exposures to this musical tradition, and evolve his own perspective as he deepens his involvement with it.

Some of the chapters of this book are abridged, updated or re-written versions of chapters from my first book: "Hindustani music — A tradition in transition". Several chapters have, however, been freshly written to ensure comprehensive coverage of the subject, and to satisfy the anticipated needs of my assumed readers.

This book omits discussion on some of the newer musical forms and formats with which Hindustani musicians have become involved over the last two decades. They are known by various names such as, East-West fusion, Sufi music, etc. The omission is not intended to deny their significance. It simply reflects the fact that they await my systematic study. The omission may also be justified because it is the orthodox formats of presenting raga-bound music, which are still dominant on the mainstream platform.

I have attempted to keep the presentation of this book reader-friendly. For readers who wish to seek a deeper understanding of the tradition, its history and its aesthetic assumptions, I have included a bibliography. The main body of the book, however, does not contain references to the listed works.

I am deeply indebted to my Guru of forty years, Pandit Arvind Parikh, for contributing a Foreword to this book. His endorsement will, I trust, deliver my work into many more hands than my labours alone might have done.

I trust this book will be as satisfying an experience for my readers as it has been for me.

Mumbai, 15 September 2011   **Deepak S. Raja**

Contents

Acknowledgements

I acknowledge my debt of gratitude to the following for making this book possible.

- The Benign Deities: Shri Vighneshwara, Shri Nataraja, and Mata Saraswati.

- The Gurus who taught me music: Shri Chandrakant Pandit (Gandharva), Shri Usman Khan Abdul Kareem Khan, Shri PB Deb Burman, Pandit Arvind Parikh, and Vidushi Dhondutai Kulkarni.

- Other guides and mentors: Dr. Sushil Kumar Saxena, Prof. Ashok Ranade, Dr. Suvarnalata Rao, Prof. N. Ramanathan, and Prof. R.C. Mehta.

- Editors who have encouraged my writings on music: N. Pattabhiraman, V Ramnarayan, Umaima Mulla-Phiroze, Vinod Mehta, M.J. Akbar, and Manoj Nair.

- Inspiring friends: Chandrakant (Chandu) Kapadia, Narain Sadhvani (Sadi), Patanjalee Amin, Anthony Raj, Namita Devidayal, Aneesh Pradhan, and Nilaksha Gupta.

- Lyle Wachovsky of India Archive Music Ltd., New York, who has supported my work in music and readily waived his copyright claims over some of the material in this book.

I acknowledge my debt of gratitude to the following for making this book possible.

- The Benign Deities: Shri Vighneshwara, Shri Nataraja, and Mata Saraswati.

- The Gurus who taught me music: Shri Chandrakant Pandit (Gandharva), Shri Usman Khan Abdul Kareem Khan, Shri PB Deb Burman, Pandit Arvind Parikh, and Vidushi Dhondutai Kulkarni.

- Other guides and mentors: Dr. Sushil Kumar Saxena, Prof. Ashok Ranade, Dr. Suvarnalata Rao, Prof. N. Ramanathan, and Prof. R.C. Mehta.

- Editors who have encouraged my writings on music: N. Pattabhiraman, V Ramnarayan, Umaima Mulla-Phiroze, Vinod Mehta, M.J. Akbar, and Manoj Nair.

- Inspiring friends: Chandrakant (Chandu) Kapadia, Narain Sadhvani (Sadi), Patanjalee Amin, Anthony Raj, Namita Devidayal, Aneesh Pradhan, and Nilaksha Gupta.

- Lyle Wachovsky of India Archive Music Ltd., New York, who has supported my work in music and readily waived his copyright claims over some of the material in this book.

- Connoisseur friends, who have scrutinised and enriched my manuscript with their suggestions: Ailsa Mathiesen (Australia), Eric Landen (USA), and Allessandro Dozio (Switzerland).

- Archivists of Hindustani music who have freely shared their treasures with me and educated me in many other ways: Prof. Rohit Desai, Shri Kishor Merchant, and Shri Bharat Jani.

- Eminent musicians who have given me interviews, and enhanced my understanding of music as well as musicianship.

1

It is "Art" Music;
not "Classical"

ention "classical music" to your neighbour
and he will look at you as if you are talking of
music from a different planet. A large part of
the blame for this lies with the word "classical" — the most
mystifying word to have entered India's musical culture.

The word "classical" was originally coined in the West
to describe any artefact which embodies the principles of
order, harmony, and reason, these being the attributes of
architecture and literature nurtured in ancient Greece and
Rome. With the progressive glorification of these values in
the West, the quality of "classicism" came to define any
work of art which represented a "standard", and which was
almost beyond criticism. A certain misdirection of meaning
occurred when the word was applied to music.

In Western music, the word "classical" refers
specifically to works composed during the "classical
period" — starting from the end of the Baroque to the
beginning of the Romanticist period. The concept covers the
works of Haydn, Mozart, Beethoven, etc. The meaning of

"classical" has been the subject of considerable debate even in the West. It now stands broadened to denote scholarly Western music, composed over the last 400-500 years. Western musicologists indoctrinated in this terminology imposed the term "classical" on Indian art music.

By any yardstick, the adjective "classical" is contextually irrelevant to Hindustani music. Besides, it is also scientifically imprecise. The accurate description is "Art" music. You can, of course, argue that as long as everyone understands what you mean by the word "classical", it does not matter what you call it. This argument is not convincing. Any word used outside its proper context tends to acquire unintended meanings. And, with respect to Indian art music, the word "classical" has certainly done so. Rather than enumerate all the misinformation carried by this word, it is more useful to consider the good sense in replacing the word "classical" with "art".

The most important connotation of "art" music is that it is a spontaneous, living, and constantly evolving expression of society's musical needs and aspirations. It is an organic part of the musical culture, and not something outside it. In short, it is not music from a different planet. It is accessible to almost anyone within the culture, though maybe with some effort.

Art music does not operate in a vacuum. Our art music has active links with at least five other segments of musical activity — primitive, folk, popular, devotional, and martial. Echoes of each category can be heard, however faintly, in all the others. Despite these interactive relationships, art music is distinct in its social function and musical features.

Features of Art Music

The artist's endeavour is guided entirely by artistic values and aesthetic purpose. The musical experience he generates is highly individualistic and abstract, far removed from the mundane and the particular. Its discipline focuses the artist's energies solely on the creation of auditory impact. The presence of non-musical stimuli (e.g. visual appeal or body language) is only incidental to the music-making process.

An art music tradition generally accommodates a variety of genres, each with its own set of rules and conventions. As a corollary, the performing tradition is always accompanied by a parallel scholarly tradition which monitors, organises, and conceptualises the trends in practice.

From audiences, art music demands a degree of respect for the music-making process, undivided attention, and an effort at appreciation. As a rule, enjoyment rises with a growing familiarity. This is indeed so because the musician has considerable freedom in applying the rules and following the conventions to the music-making. His compliance may be literal, imaginative, liberal, oblique, eccentric or even defiant. A vast range of possibilities is what makes it an art.

Appreciating Hindustani Music

People gravitate towards art music for a variety of reasons, and sometimes even accidentally. What they discover in it is the possibility of a richer emotional life. In any society, those who value such satisfactions are few. This is why the audience for art music is generally small. Those who enter this world successfully are those who have the basic equipment required for receiving its signals, and have cultivated an ability to interpret them in a manner that is personally meaningful.

A widely cited, though simplistic, definition of music is "structured sound". The task of understanding any form of music then breaks down into two components — understanding the sound, and understanding the structure. Art music has a small audience simply because its sounds and its structures are more complex than other forms of music, and a majority of the populace lacks either the basic equipment or the motivation to cultivate an understanding of them.

For understanding the sounds, a listener needs the ability for differentiating one note from another. The more astute this ability, the sharper will be a person's perception of the melodic contours and ornamentations of art music. The melodic contour is, however, only the basic level of sound patterns in Hindustani music. At the next level, the listener has to decipher the giant matrix of melodic contours called a raga.

Beyond the melody, he has to understand the patterns embedded in the pre-composed form called a bandish, along with rhythmic pattern called the tala. Alongside, he has to comprehend the melodic and rhythmic patterns underlying the improvisations deployed by the musician in the process of delivering the raga experience. And, finally, he has to understand the overall architecture of the genre within which the entire process of music-making takes place. Once the "big picture" is evident even hazily to the listener, the aesthetic and emotional intent of the musician begins to reveal itself.

In effect, then, we are talking of three kinds of equipment a person needs in decent measure to appreciate Hindustani music — differentiation between notes, pattern recognition, and emotional receptivity.

Pitch differentiation is probably a genetically determined faculty. Some people are highly sensitive to the intervals between notes, while others are less sensitive. Total insensitivity is rare. The second — pattern recognition — is a cerebral proclivity, which is more abundant than pitch differentiation, and can also be cultivated. The third — emotional receptivity — is widely understood as being partly a personality dimension, and partly a stage-of-life-cycle phenomenon. Most people would believe that this faculty cannot be cultivated. But, culture aficionados believe that it can be cultivated at any stage of life, and this should indeed be one of the objectives of encouraging people to expose themselves to art music.

If, by whatever process, and for whatever reason, you feel drawn towards Hindustani music, you can probably assume that you possess the

basic equipment and eligibility for its appreciation. The only thing that remains is cultivating the familiarity with the sounds and patterns. This cannot be achieved by reading books. Decades of training with a competent Guru is not the only alternative — though it helps. Your purpose can be achieved by an extensive study of recordings, and attendance at concerts. And, once you have become a connoisseur, you also gain personal access to the leading musicians. Interacting with exceptional musical minds can often give you unimaginably delightful insights into the secrets of music.

Connoisseurship is a coveted status amongst music lovers, and this is why some people invest substantial amounts of time in its pursuit. But, everybody does not have to become a connoisseur. The joys of pursuit keep growing along with the maturation of understanding. And, understanding keeps rising with constant involvement. So, there are rewards for anyone who walks along this path.

2

Vehicles of
the Raga Experience

Hindustani music is synonymous with raga music. The primary aim of a performance is delivering the raga experience. To enable the musician to organise all the facets of music in consonance with his vision of the raga, the tradition permits him the combined role of composer and performer.

Despite this convergence of roles, his freedom is not unlimited. His individuality and creativity need to function within the various frameworks provided by the tradition. These frameworks channellise his creative energies towards achieving his artistic aims, while also protecting his audiences against the risk of bewilderment. Great musicians do, of course, create new — and sometimes mystifying — frameworks for expressing their musical ideas. If such creations find sufficient acceptance with audiences and other musicians, the tradition either gets modified, or is enlarged to accommodate such innovations.

The available frameworks are of varying flexibility, and govern a musician's efforts towards making the desired

impact. The basic frameworks to understand are: the raga (driver of melody), the tala (driver of rhythm), the bandish (integrator of melody, rhythm and poetry), and the genre (the organiser of musical material).

The Raga as Melodic Framework

In the formalistic genres, such as Dhrupad and Khayal, the choice of a raga is the basic decision a musician has to make. The raga is, indeed, the most flexible framework — the most formless form — available to the musician. Aptly, it has been said that anyone who succeeds in defining the notion of a raga, has almost certainly failed to understand it. This is why there are, and will always be, as many definitions of it as there are authors. It is sufficient here to consider the two main approaches.

The theoretical view is that a raga is a set of rules governing the selection, sequencing, and treatment of notes. All melodic patterns conforming to these rules will be aesthetically coherent and avoid the risk of confusion with other ragas. Empiricists, however, take a different view. While admitting to the vast improvisational potential of a raga, they point out that every raga has a well-established skeletal phraseology which recurs intermittently during a rendition, and distinguishes the raga from others. They therefore prefer to understand a raga as a distinctive melodic matrix/framework or as a partially pre-composed melodic entity. Both these approaches are valuable because they offer different perspectives, without really contradicting each other.

How many ragas does a musician choose from? Approximately 1000 ragas of known or documented grammar are believed to exist. Of these, about 150 are in circulation at any particular time. Very few musicians would know more than 50 ragas well. And, most are really comfortable with performing only 25/30 ragas. Having decided which raga he wishes to perform, a musician has to choose the genre in which he wishes to perform it.

The Genres as Presentation Framework

Though a genre in Hindustani music has several defining features, it is defined most conspicuously by its architecture — the manner of organising the musical material. Contemporary Hindustani music corresponds broadly to the structural models of Dhrupad, Khayal and Thumree. In vocal music, these genres are present in their distinctive form, while in instrumental music, elements of two or more genres could be blended. In addition to their distinctive presentation formats, however, the different genres also have their distinctive moods.

Theoretically, any raga can be performed in any genre. But, aesthetic compatibility causes some ragas to be performed in some genres more than others. Romantic ragas like Bhairavi, Kafi and Khamaj, for instance, are encountered mostly in the Thumree genre, but hardly ever in the Khayal genre. Likewise, the profound ragas like Darbari Kanada or Puriya will be heard in the Dhrupad or Khayal genres, but never in the Thumree genre. There are very few ragas, like Jhinjhoti or Desh, which feature in all the three major genres.

Within the chosen genre, the musician has then to choose the composition, called the bandish.

The Bandish as the Pre-composed Framework

The word "bandish" comes from the Sanskrit "bandhan" = binding. And, this is what the bandish does. It is pre-composed with the purpose of binding the melodic, rhythmic, and poetic elements (where relevant) into a self-contained piece of music. The bandish becomes the nucleus around which the musician builds his improvisations to shape the raga experience. The bandish thus also holds the totality of the rendition together.

How much choice does a musician have in bandishes? In each genre, the popular ragas would offer a wider choice of bandishes, while rare ragas would offer a smaller choice. Some ragas are, indeed, so rare that, in living memory, only one or two bandishes are known to have been performed in

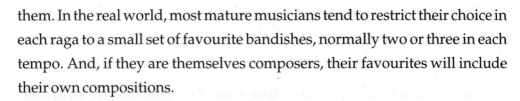

them. In the real world, most mature musicians tend to restrict their choice in each raga to a small set of favourite bandishes, normally two or three in each tempo. And, if they are themselves composers, their favourites will include their own compositions.

The Tala as the Rhythmic Framework

The tala is a cyclical entity. Being a calibration of time, it is a totally binding discipline for the musician. Every tala (rhythmic cycle) has a specific number of beats, and has subdivisions, which may be symmetrical or asymmetrical. The subdivision pattern imparts to each tala its distinctive cadence. The melodic-poetic lines of the bandish will correspond to one or more iterations of the tala cycle. Like ragas, talas also have their individual moods defined by their cadential patterns.

How many talas does Hindustani music have? Tala literature over a century will probably document over 50 talas. But, a survey of contemporary practice might deliver less than 30 talas, of which about 12 will account for over 90 per cent of performances across all genres. Like ragas, talas also have their special territories, and conventions substantially guide practice. So, the width of choice in talas for a particular rendition is almost academic.

Chautal (12 beats), Dhamar (14 beats) and Sula Tala (10 beats) are "patent" talas of contemporary Dhrupad. In slow-tempo Khayal vocalism, you are likely to encounter Ektal (12 beats), Jhoomra (14 beats), Tilwada (16 beats) and Tritala (16 beats). In medium-tempo Khayal, you could hear Jhaptala (10 beats), and Rupak (7 beats). In brisk-tempo Khayal, you will generally hear Tritala (16 beats) or Ektala (12 beats). In Thumree vocal renditions, you could hear Deepchandi (14 beats) in medium tempo, but occasionally also the minor talas like Dadra (6 beats) or Keherva (8 beats) or a Tritala variant (16 beats). In the music of the string instruments — Sitar, Sarod, Santoor — you will generally hear Tritala in slow-tempo, Jhaptala or

Rupak in medium-tempo, and Tritala again or sometimes Ektala, in brisk tempo. On the wind and bow instruments, which largely follow the vocal idiom, the deployment of talas tends to be similar to the vocal Khayal and Thumree.

But, if you are listening to Ali Akbar Khan, the Sarod wizard, you could well encounter his own rhythmic creations in 9½, 11½ and 13½ beats, which will challenge the finest Tabla accompanist he could find.

A musician chooses his raga, his genre, his bandish in a specific tala, his tempo of rendition — all with one single objective. That is, to deliver the raga experience. What constitutes the raga experience?

The Raga Experience

In Sanskrit, the word "raga" does not have any melodic connotation at all. Its only connotation is emotional. The raga in music is a highly evolved and potent melodic trigger for an emotional response. This relates to the notion of "rasa" (literally: essence) linked inseparably to the raga in the Indian tradition.

The psycho-acoustics of ragas are beyond the scope of this discussion. Suffice it to appreciate that each melodic entity (raga) is capable of eliciting a certain range of emotional responses. The artistic aim of every rendition is to unleash the emotional charge latent in the melody, and to elicit a response.

The notion of music as a language for communicating emotions is, of course, a much debated subject. To the Indian mind, however, the debate is, a priori, pointless. Here we come face-to-face with the inherent transcendentalism of Hindu thought. The Indian aesthetic tradition views sensory experience as a pathway to the emotional, and the emotional as a pathway to the spiritual. All art is, therefore, validated by a dominant criterion — its ability to elicit an emotional response. This criterion acknowledges that, at its most intense, the experience of beauty is a near-mystical experience. This defines the potential of the artistic endeavour, and its reception, for personality transformation and spiritual evolution.

3

Raga Bhairav at Midnight!
The Time Theory of Ragas

hairav, a sunrise raga, being performed at midnight is totally unacceptable to a majority of Indian connoisseurs. But, the time may have come for them to take a more relaxed view on the time-related propriety for the performance of ragas.

In Hindustani music, every raga is prescribed for performance during a specific three-hour time-slot of the twenty-four hour daily cycle. Western musicologists have, for long, described this facet of India's musical culture as fanciful and arbitrary. For performing musicians, scholarly scepticism is, of course, not a major issue. What concerns them and the impresarios of the music world is the question Indian music lovers are now asking in significant numbers. They want to know why the timings of concerts — generally between sunset and midnight — should limit the variety of ragas they hear on the concert platform.

There are other arguments, too, for this convention to be revisited. Carnatic music, a product of the same tradition as Hindustani music, does not follow any such prescription. Secondly, inside a modern auditorium, environmental

conditions are identical at any time of the day and throughout the year. Finally, there is no way of controlling the time of the day or night, or part of the year, during which audiences will listen to pre-recorded music, which is now the primary vehicle of music globally. So, the time-theory could also be headed for redundancy.

Despite the unresolved issues surrounding the time theory, significant Hindustani musicians have not so far deviated blatantly from its prescriptions on Indian soil. With uninitiated Indians and aliens dominating their global audience, such deviations could begin soon. We have, therefore, to develop, if possible, a rational perspective for resolving the imminent conflicts between conventional notions of artistic propriety, and emerging conditions.

There is no wisdom in accepting traditional prescriptions just because they can be assumed to represent the accumulated wisdom of society. It is equally unwise to reject them outright because we do not have access to their original logic. It is in this spirit that the time theory needs to be examined.

Raga and Rasa

The fundamental concept in Indian aesthetics is rasa. Rasa refers to the specific emotional state that any artistic endeavour elicits, communicates, or reflects. Every raga is a tool by which the musician maximises the possibility of eliciting the target emotional response from his audiences. The tradition has assumed a correspondence between a raga (a melodic structure) and its rasa (emotional content) based on its experience and general acceptance.

The experience also suggests that each raga has the highest probability of eliciting the candidate emotional response during certain hours of the day/night or during certain seasons of the year. Thus has evolved a performing tradition, which assumes, broadly, a three-way correspondence between melodic patterns (ragas), emotional states (rasas) and environmental and climatic variables.

Many non-musical factors do, of course, influence our receptivity and response to a musical presentation. But, a musician can only control musical variables; and this is what the tradition helps him to do. In doing so, the tradition attempts to harmonise musical variables with environmental variables, based on its understanding of the relationship between the two. At the root of these prescriptions is also the oriental notion that man is most effective when he acts in concert with nature, rather than in discord with it.

Arbitrary as these prescriptions may appear, they relate music to a reality whose relevance recent researches in physiology are beginning to vindicate. The hypothesis is that our bodily and emotional states respond constantly to changes in the quality of sunlight, and climatic factors such as humidity and temperature. If this proposition has any merit, it is plausible that there should also be specific environmental conditions most conducive to different categories of emotional experience. Our performing tradition has attempted to stabilise its understanding of these probabilities with the benefit of centuries of trial and error.

This configuration of ideas came closer to "scientific" respectability in the first quarter of the twentieth century, when the pioneering musicologist, V.N. Bhatkhande observed a relationship between raga scales and their time-specific prescriptions. Since then, other scholars and musicians have identified additional patterns, which provide some support for the time-theory of ragas as an evolved parameter in the classification matrix.

A Rational Perspective

The theory, as understood so far, falls short of being a comprehensive and fully organised system of relationships. Some psychometric experiments have been conducted to verify the association of melodic patterns with time-slots in the audience mind. The results are, so far, tentative in their affirmation. It is impossible to predict whether a more ambitious enquiry will ever be attempted, or will even be conclusive.

Quite irrespective of what scientific approaches might reveal about these psycho-acoustic assumptions, they will not change the way different people relate to music. The "believers" may, therefore, have to accept that, maybe, the theory works for them because they have Indian bodies, and Indian minds, of a particular generation, responding under the sunlight quality and climatic conditions characteristic of the Indian subcontinent.

The generational issue might be more important than it seems. Generations brought up on pre-recorded music, and accustomed to attending concerts in environmentally engineered auditoria, may be relatively insensitive to the spirit of the time theory, and consequently unsympathetic to it.

Climatic conditions, too, cannot be an insignificant factor. If the Hindustani and Carnatic traditions are derived from a common source, the time theory was probably common to them until their bifurcation. Why did the Carnatic tradition abandon the theory, while the Hindustani tradition retained it? It can be hypothesised that, by virtue of being closer to the equator, the southern states experience a far lower level of variation in climatic conditions within the day and between the different seasons than the northern, non-peninsular, states do. This could be the reason why the Raga Hindolam/Malkauns does not suggest, to Carnatic audiences, as radical a contrast with the Raga Bhairavi/Hanumatodi in aesthetic value and emotional content, as it does to Hindustani audiences.

Once we appreciate this logic, it can be extended farther. A Midnight Sonata composed in Raga Bhairav by a Scandinavian composer need not raise eyebrows, because a Scandinavian's physiological and psychological relationship with sunlight is radically different from ours.

As Hindustani music addresses an increasingly diverse global audience, the musician becomes progressively incapable of controlling the time and environmental conditions attendant to the performance. The context of the musical experience is now undergoing a fundamental transformation in terms of audience profiles, the media of delivery and environmental conditions. A degree of "de-contextualisation" now seems inevitable. The emerging context may oblige conservative connoisseurs to loosen their strictures further.

Why should it be wrong for an Indian to perform Raga Bhairav at the Darbari hour, but okay for a Scandinavian to do so?

Those who cannot make such an attitudinal transition could soon find themselves in an indignant minority. The emerging reality will not show any deference to whether their conservatism is subjective or objective; rational or irrational. It will confront them with a choice between the dissonance of concert-attendance and the comfort of "proper" enjoyment of music through pre-recorded media at home.

4

The Gharanas in Hindustani Music

In conversations about Hindustani music, you often come across mention of a vocalist being from the ABC Gharana, or a sitarist being from the XYZ Gharana. What is it all about? How did it all begin, and what does it mean today?

The word "gharana" denotes a distinctive style of rendering raga-based music, especially in the modern genres. The gharanas had their forerunners in the four "banis" (literally, dialects) of medieval Dhrupad music (fifteenth-eighteenth centuries). But, even pre-Dhrupad music recognised several "mats" (literally, ideologies), acknowledging the existence of diversity.

The notion of stylistic diversity corresponding to the idea of gharanas has been most well defined in vocal music, and has dominated the Hindustani scene until the nineteenth century. However, the model is also applicable to some streams of instrumental music such as the Sitar and the Sarod, which have a reasonably long histroy of evolution.

Stylistic diversity is fundamental to Indian culture because of the large number of racial-ethnic-linguistic

groups that inhabit the subcontinent. Some homogeneity was probably achieved during the Mughal era, when a large number of musician communities were concentrated in and around Delhi. When the Mughal Empire disintegrated, they migrated in hordes to smaller principalities in search of alternative patronage. Once art music intermingled with the regional cultures under conditions of geographical isolation, the essential diversity of India re-surfaced, and got crystallised in the form of gharanas.

Considering the powerful forces favouring diversity, it is remarkable that the core of Hindustani music remained uniform throughout India, and stable for centuries. The diversity we encounter is manifested largely in the manner of rendition. This diversity needed names for identification. The word "gharana" emerged as the most appropriate for this purpose.

The Origin of Gharanas

The word "gharana" is derived from ghar (house/home, from the Sanskrit noun: griha). In Hindi and Urdu, "gharana" is a collective noun denoting those who live under the same roof; therefore, a family, a lineage, a clan. The names of gharanas are most commonly the names of places, such as Agra, Rampur, Gwalior, etc. The naming of gharanas after places thus implicitly attributes its distinguishing features to the place of origin. Gharanas are also always associated with landmark personalities.

Thus, we have three different, historical factors, converging to define a gharana as a stylistic lineage. In plain language, once upon a time, there was a great musician, whose music was different from those who lived in other villages or cities. He groomed his sons as musicians and they sang a lot like him; and their music was also different from the music of those who lived in other places, and in the same respect as their father's was. And, this went on for several generations, as long as conditions were favourable.

Favourable Conditions

It is easy to appreciate the appearance of a great musician who influenced many other musicians of his own generation as well as the next. But, this leaves some unanswered questions. Why did the sons of musicians need, or want, to become musicians? And, why did the style of a musician from Gwalior, and his sons and nephews, need to be, or end up becoming, distinctly different from that of their corresponding generations from Agra or Patiala?

Hereditary musicianship was a creation of genetic as well as economic factors. Genetic factors were conducive, within limits, to the transmission of the musical sensibility. Familial factors ensured a great deal of involuntarily learning. The voluntary aspect responded to the attractions of feudal patronage.

Employment by princes and aristocrats promised lifelong security, and constituted the most attractive market for musicians. An effort to bequeath patronage thus constituted intelligent career-planning for their children, considering the paucity of formal education, and limited career options offered by a backward economy. This strategy had a good chance of success if they could turn their children into their own musical clones. This process struck deep roots in the musical culture because feudal patrons rewarded its products. A king could legitimately boast of his army, his elephants, his jewels, his palaces, and even his gharana of music.

Even without its cloning intentions, hereditary musicianship would have been eminently suitable for the transmission of the Hindustani tradition, which combines the roles of composer and performer. Involuntary familial exposure during the formative years, accompanied by voluntary submission to the rigours of grooming, was therefore uniquely convenient as a familial model.

Predictably, heredity proved to be an unreliable source of musicianship potential. Patrons obliged eminent musicians to groom promising talent outside the orbit of kinship. But, since the nature of the art demanded intensive exposure, and the "market" demanded stylistic continuity, the mentor-pupil relationship cast itself into the parent-child model of co-habitation, and total subordination verging on servility.

The system attempted cloning. But, change inevitably crept in, thanks to three human imperfections — imperfect perception, imperfect retention, and imperfect reproduction. The bias towards continuity resulted in the progressive refinement of the salient features of its style, in addition to giving the music a greater degree of coherence. These processes yielded a variety of musical styles defined by a genealogy of tutelage, only partially coinciding with heredity.

Such an outcome was possible because of the relative insulation of each lineage from others. Additional protection against dilution came from the dogmatic attitudes cultivated during the period of grooming. These fortifications worked because of the backwardness of the country in terms of transport and communications.

The gharanas thus came to be distinctive stylistic lineages of post-Dhrupad art music, shaped by feudal patronage, heredity, a rigorous pedagogical environment, and a backward economy starved of education, career options, transport and communications. The result they delivered was a variety of distinct musical styles, with each style possessing a distinctive set of assiduously cultivated musical values.

Chinks in the Armour

By mid-twentieth century, it was observed that the greatest vocalists of the late-nineteenth/early twentieth century had been, almost without exception, disciples of multiple gharanas. Evidently, stylistic loyalty to a single gharana could, under certain conditions, be an inhibitor of exceptional potential in so highly individualistic an art. Chinks in the gharana armour expanded into gaping holes starting from the dawn of the twentieth century, when the print and electronic media intervened.

In the first quarter of the century, V.N. Bhatkhande and Vishnu Digambar Paluskar published encyclopaedic documentation of the Hindustani tradition. Paluskar, however, made a more immediate impact on the accessibility of musical knowledge and performing skills by setting up Gandharva Mahavidyalaya, India's first music university. In its early years, this university trained a veritable army of musical missionaries to run music schools all over the country. Their work partially liberated music education from purely aural transmission and from the tyranny of the teacher-taught relationship. These developments weakened the forces which created the "cloning effect" characteristic of the gharana phenomenon.

The forces supporting stylistic diversity were further weakened by the growth of the radio and the gramophone record around the same time. They made the music of every musician accessible to every other musician and aspirant to musicianship. By the time the cost-effective audio-cassette made its appearance with concert-length recordings in the 1960s, pre-recorded music was emerging as a "virtual Guru". Hereafter, technology and commerce worked in tandem to demolish traditional barriers to the acquisition of musical knowledge and skills, to talent's entry into musicianship, and to the public's access to music.

However, even before this development, independence had demolished the bulwark of the gharana system — the feudal aristocracy. Along with the patron class, this transition also wiped out an important quality control mechanism operating in Hindustani music. In the feudal era, only the finest musicians secured aristocratic patronage. Their status automatically attracted the most promising talent in the territory as disciples. This matching of talent to opportunity took a beating when the princely states were abolished.

Democratic India forced musicians to migrate from the smaller towns to the big cities. Economic development started offering their children alternative careers. A talent-based (sometimes resources-based) entry of aspirants began to replace heredity. But, the anonymity of urban life could not guarantee the gravitation of the most promising aspirants towards the greatest musicianship. Even when this did happen, the stresses of self-employment left the greatest musicians devoid of energy and time for teaching. The rigorous process of personalised tutoring, that had sustained the gharana institution in the feudal context, succumbed to urbanisation.

These factors, coupled with easier access to music through the electronic media, corroded the two most important features of the gharana system — stylistic distinctiveness of each gharana from others, and aesthetic coherence of the music shaped within each gharana. Bonnie Wade of Berkeley University, an authority on this subject, observed in 1984 that the epitaph for the gharanas of Khayal vocalism was about to be written. Though unintended, this observation held true for stylistic lineages in all segments of Hindustani music.

The Gharanas Today

Gharanas are now little more than misleading — sometimes treacherous — history for audiences, and an academic indulgence for critics. This truth calls for neither lament, nor rejoicing. Hindustani music is built on the foundations of continuity within change. This reality will remain operative as long as Hindustani music remains an improvisation-dominant tradition, impossible to transmit without a personalised apprenticeship. The same is true of stylistic diversity. It existed before the gharanas emerged, and will remain as long as India remains a multi-racial, multi-ethnic, multi-linguistic subcontinent.

With the fading away of the gharanas, one model of art transmission is being replaced by an alternative model, or perhaps a multiplicity of models. Some emerging models might even appear to favour the forces of homogenisation and ossification rater than sustaining the forces of diversity and change. A "mega-trend", if any, is however not yet clear enough to be conceptualised. In the future, as in the past, the balance between continuity and change, and between homogeneity and diversity, will be decided by how audiences want art music to respond to their musical needs.

5

Dhrupad
A Cultural Enigma

If the history of the Dhrupad genre is written in 2050, it will have to reckon with the credible musicianship and scholarly contributions of several Europeans and Americans, along with a few Indians. Dhrupad is fast becoming a Western genre of Indian origin, performed predominantly for Western audiences by Indians and, increasingly, also by Western musicians.

The term Dhrupad (Dhruva = immutable/fixed + Pada = Hymn/verse) refers to a genre of raga-based music which dominated Hindustani music between the fifteenth and the eighteenth centuries. Because of the poetic bias of the genre, Dhrupad has its moorings in vocal music. However, instrumental music, mainly the Rudra Veena (popularly known as the Been), has also been an integral part of the genre.

The genre has its roots in the devotional music traditionally performed in the Vaishnava temples of northern India. Its migration to the secular environment of the feudal courts as an art form was accompanied by a diversification of its poetic content, and a great deal of sophistication in its presentation. The Golden Age of Dhrupad commenced when Emperor Akbar (Reign: 1542-1605), invited the legendary Miya Tansen to the Imperial Court. From Delhi, its influence spread far and wide. At its zenith, Dhrupad held sway over the whole of non-peninsular India. While Dhrupad was still at its peak, a variety of pre-Dhrupad and Middle-Eastern musical influences were coalescing to shape the rival Khayal genre.

Nasir Aminuddin Dagar and Nasir Moinuddin Dagar

In the sunset years of the Mughal Empire, leading musicians — so far concentrated in Delhi and its neighbour-hood — began migrating to smaller principalities. This not only created new centres of Dhrupad music, but also exposed Dhrupad musicians to a diverse environment. In their new environs, many lineages of Dhrupad musicians diverted their energies to the Khayal genre, and spearheaded its ascendancy over the receding Dhrupad genre.

By the time of India's Independence, Dhrupad was often described as "a museum piece". This was more true of the art of the Rudra Veena, than of the vocal art. Dhrupad vocalism could then still boast of a sizeable resource of quality musicianship. Even amongst Khayal singers, Dhrupad had remained, till then, relevant as an essential part of training — the repository of the sciences of breath control and intonation. It was this resource which enabled a revival.

The revival, such as is evident, was fuelled by the following Dhrupad acquired in Europe, starting from the mid-1960s. It began when the Indologist, Alain Danielou, with UNESCO support, introduced the pre-eminent vocalists, Nasir Aminuddin and Nasir Moinuddin Dagar, to Europe. Dhrupad's burgeoning international constituency stimulated a substantial inflow of fresh talent to the genre. By the end of the twentieth century, Dhrupad vocalism could boast of a small group of musicians who were credible at home, but were dependent increasingly on the Western market for their livelihood.

Styles in Dhrupad Music

Authoritative medieval texts mention the four "banis" or styles of Dhrupad music. These classifications were evidently based on the language/dialect in which the verses were written: In later years, the four banis came to signify stylistic distinctions.

Although contemporary Dhrupad musicians profess allegiance to one of the four "banis" through their lineages, the stylistic distinctions between them are no longer discernible. This is easily explained. With the steady shrinkage in

Gundecha Brothers
Umakant and Ramakant Gundecha

the number of Dhrupad practitioners, aspirants have obviously had to draw musical ideas, perhaps   even unselectively, from a multiplicity of sources. In addition, Dhrupad needs to adapt itself to contemporary audience tastes in order to remain relevant. As a result, the only viable classification in contemporary Dhrupad vocalism is, broadly, between the aggressive styles and the relatively softer styles.

The Structure of Dhrupad Presentation

Raga presentation in the Dhrupad genre has a simple and transparent structure, especially when compared to the modern Khayal. A typical Dhrupad presentation has two components:

(1)   An alap (prelude) which is rendered solo, without any poetic content, and without percussion accompaniment. The alap goes through three stages — slow tempo, medium tempo, and brisk tempo.

(2)   A pada (verse) rendered to percussion accompaniment, along with melodic and rhythmic improvisations. The tempo of percussion accompaniment is generally stable throughout the rendition. The verse could be composed in any of the talas accepted in the Dhrupad genre.

A durational analysis of Dhrupad performances establishes the three-tiered alap as consuming over 60 per cent of the duration of a raga presentation. Presentations in Dhamar and the minor rhythmic cycles may, however, frequently devote a lower share of duration to the alap.

The Dhrupad Experience

In addition to the differences in the architecture, Dhrupad vocalism is qualitatively different from the more popular Khayal genre because of its ensemble and its rhythmic canvas.

The ensemble for Dhrupad performance is austere. It consists of a pair of Tanpuras as the acoustic ambience, and Pakhawaj (a barrel drum) as percussion accompaniment. Been accompaniment for vocal performances, once the norm, is now rare. Unlike their Khayal counterparts, Dhupad vocalists, as a rule, stay away from Sarangi or Harmonium accompaniment.

Dhrupad traditionally deployed a wide variety of rhythmic cycles, some of which are also encountered in Khayal vocalism. Perhaps in its desire to differentiate itself more categorically from Khayal, contemporary Dhrupad

mainly deploys Chautala (12 beats), Dhamar (14 beats), and Sulatala (10 beats).

Gharanas of Dhrupad

Though scholars recognise five gharanas or stylistic lineages of Dhrupad as being in existence, only the first three listed here are represented on the concert platform.

(a) The Dagar Gharana: This is the oldest gharana of Dhrupad, having been founded by Nayak Haridas Dagar in the sixteenth century. Its descendants converted to Islam during the eighteenth century. In recent times, its most eminent representatives have been vocalists, Nasir Moinuddin Dagar (1919-66) and Nasir Aminuddin Dagar (1923-2002) and the Been maestro, Zia Mohiuddin Dagar (1929-90). The music of the lineage tends towards the softer style of rendition.

(b) The Darbhanga Gharana: This gharana was founded in the eighteenth century by two brothers, whose descendants have carried the "Mallik" surname. In the post-Independence era, the most distinguished musicians of this lineage have been Ramchatur Mallik (1906-90) and Vidur Mallik (1936-2002). The music of this lineage tends towards the more aggressive style of rendition.

(c) The Bettiya Gharana: Founded in the seventeenth century, it wielded tremendous influence over Dhrupad in the entire eastern region. Bettiya is represented, on the contemporary concert platform, by Indrakishore Mishra (born: 1957). In its current manifestation, the music of this lineage follows a middle path, with a mild inclination towards the aggressive.

(d) The Talwandi Gharana: This gharana originated in north-west India, now in Pakistan, and is currently based in Lahore. Very little is known about its contemporary musicianship or style.

(e) The Mathura Gharana: This is the oldest gharana of Haveli Sangeet, the Dhrupad tradition of the Vaishnava temples. Though its members have stepped out of the temples, their art has not made a complete transition to the elaborate format of contempo-rary art music Dhrupad.

Uday Bhawalkar

Dhrupad Today

Dhrupad probably declined in popularity because of its resistance to change, restrictions on individual creativity, and its failure to accommodate changing audience tastes. Comprehensive raga presentation in Hindustani music needed to avert extinction. It did so by loosening the rigid Dhrupad format, and found a ready solution in the already mature rival, the Khayal genre.

Some Dhrupad gharanas, however, resisted the Khayal wave. Thanks to their tenacity, the genre now stands partially restored to the mainstream. Their exertions appear to be winning back mature Hindustani audiences who had not heard quality Dhrupad for a long time. For the younger audiences, Dhrupad is a novel experience, but structurally more accessible than Khayal.

In creating an audience for their music, today's Dhrupad vocalists have successfully targeted audiences nurtured in the Carnatic tradition. In south India, Dhrupad is making a headway because of two factors: a growing receptivity of Carnatic-oriented audiences to Hindustani music, and the similarity of the Dhrupad format to some presentation formats in Carnatic music.

In the domestic music market, audience preferences or loyalties are shaped by individual musicianship and not as much by the genre. In Europe and the US, on the other hand, there appears to be a genre-based, almost cult-like, following for Dhrupad, though of course, only quality musicianship is acceptable even amongst these audiences. Never before has a genre of art music been pronounced dead in India, experienced so shaky a revival with home audiences, and become popular enough with alien audiences to become so largely dependent on them. This makes Dhrupad one of the cultural enigmas of our times.

6

Khayal Vocalism
Welcome to the Xerox Gharanas

The next time you attend a vocal music concert, there is a good chance that you will hear either an Amir Khan Xerox, a Bhimsen Joshi Xerox, a Kishori Amonkar Xerox, or a Kumar Gandharva Xerox. Such an observation would have been indefensible only 50 years ago. Today, many connoisseurs will find themselves nodding in agreement.

The vast scope the Khayal provided for individuality was predominantly responsible for its ascendency over the Dhrupad genre. The name itself tells a large part of the story. The word "Khayal" is of Perso-Arabic origin, and has been variously translated as idea, imagination, subjectivity, individuality, and impression. All these meanings are consistent with the character of the genre. Social, cultural and technological forces are, however, fast erasing the individualism of the genre and threatening the stylistic diversity once on offer.

Amongst north Indian genres of vocal music, the Khayal is, without doubt, the one that "provides its performers the greatest opportunity and challenge to display the depth and breadth of musical knowledge and skills. Its essence lies in the manner in which artists take the characteristics that distinguish Khayal as a genre, make those choices that lie within their group traditions, summon their own creative individuality, and create a unique Khayal at each performance."

— Wade, Bonnie C., Khyal: Creativity within
North India's Classical Music Tradition,
Cambridge University Press, 1st edn. 1984

The Ascendancy of the Khayal

The "medieval" Dhrupad, and the "modern" Khayal genre, have been contemporaries for almost the entire period of Dhrupad dominance. Dhrupad evolved as a highly formal and disciplined art form with a strong

Amir Khan

pre-composed tendency. The Khayal evolved, in parallel, as a predominantly improvised form, and a vehicle for individual creativity.

Scholars trace the Khayal genre to the Rupakalapti form of vocal music in practice since the eighth/ninth centuries. In the thirteenth century, the mystic-poet-musician Amir Khusro, apparently gave it a Perso-Arabic name, introduced it to the patronage of Muslim rulers, and encouraged its practice amongst singers of Qawwali, a form of sufi music. The present-day Khayal thus represents a fusion of older Indian musical formats with Perso-Arabic influences starting from the thirteenth century. The genre acquired some stature under the patronage of the Sharqui Sultans of Jaunpur (fifteenth century), and attained maturity and sophistication during the reign of Emperor Mohammad Shah of Delhi (eighteenth century). Starting around this time, the Khayal steadily pushed Dhrupad off centrestage.

The Changing Character of the Khayal

Mohan Nadkarni, the veteran music critic, described the Khayal's character as "formal aloofness". In this description, he captured both the salient features of the genre which distinguish it from the other major vocal genres — Dhrupad and Thumree. Formalism refers to the distinctive structure and architecture of the Khayal. And, aloofness is a matter of stance and demeanour, which makes the Khayal elicit an emotional response, without explicitly soliciting it. Dhrupad is far more formalistic than the Khayal — it is commanding and authoritative. Thumree is the opposite of aloof — it is intimate and even seductive.

Kishori Amonkar

The last quarter of the twentieth century witnessed a revolt against both these facets of the Khayal's personality. The revolt is reflected in the musical tendencies of three immensely influential vocalists — Kishori Amonkar, Kumar Gandharva, and Jasraj. Amongst these, Kishori Amonkar has remained fastidiously faithful to the structural formalism of the Khayal genre, while pushing it towards the intimacy of the Thumree. Jasraj's revolt is mild against formalism, and bold against its aloofness. Kumar Gandharva's revolt was comprehensive, having departed from formalism as well as aloofness.

V.H. Deshpande, an influential musicologist, sees in these developments the dawn of romanticism in Hindustani music. Arising from the success of these luminaries, romanticism is now on the march, while classicism is marginalised, awaiting the emergence of a new class of audiences for its revival.

The Gharanas of Khayal Vocalism

It is natural that the highly individualistic Khayal genre should have encouraged a considerable diversity of styles in the rendition of raga-based music. Several such distinctive styles emerged within the broad framework of the Khayal genre during the colonial era, mostly under the patronage of feudal principalites. These gharanas are named either after the principalities where they were cultivated, or the founder's home-town or village.

Bhimsen Joshi

Authoritaties on this subject (V.H. Deshpande and Bonnie Wade) have recognised the following gharanas as distinctive stylistic lineages of Khayal music.

1. Gwalior Gharana: The last towering vocalist of this tradition was Omkarnath Thakur.

2. Agra Gharana: The tallest vocalist of this tradition was Faiyyaz Khan.

3. Jaipur–Atrauli Gharana: The most celebrated twentieth-century vocalist of this gharana was Kesarbai Kerkar.

4. Patiala Gharana: This gharana is symbolised by the vocalism of Bade Ghulam Ali Khan.

5. Indore/Bhindi Bazar Gharana: This gharana is recognised largely by the musicianship of Amir Khan.

6. Kairana Gharana: This gharana is identified with Abdul Kareem Khan, its founder.

7. Rampur-Sahaswan Gharana: In recent times, Mushtaq Hussain Khan has been the most distinguished vocalists of the gharanas.

Deshpande cautioned enlightened opinion against glorifying the gharanas and placing an undue premium on stylistic conformity amongst its followers. He pointed out, with stunning validity, that the greatest vocalists in pre-Independence India, almost without exception, acquired their art from more than one gharana or Guru, and openly credited their accomplishments to the multiplicity of influences. Conformity with the tradition, he appears to suggest, has no value without originality.

Kumar Gandharva

Stylistic Diversity

By following different music-making philosophies, and nurturing different specialisations, the erstwhile gharanas collectively offered a wide choice of mature musical experiences to their audiences. Their presence could be felt till the 1960s, after which it began to recede. By the time of this writing, Khayal gharanas have drifted into history. Consequently, the concert platform now features very few vocalists, whose music is rooted in the stylistic hallmarks of any of the major gharanas. These forces have had their predictable consequences for the stylistic variety on offer.

Traditional grooming was not, by any stretch of imagination, a Xerox machine. The well-groomed products of the system not only acquired the musical content and style of the lineage, but also its thought process, and its philosophy of music-making. This led to a maturity in the communication of musical ideas, aesthetic coherence, and the flowering of originality.

With the present-day scarcity of traditional grooming, most aspirants have no access to the "process" of music-making. But, thanks to the ample availability of recorded music and poorly trained Gurus, the talented and the determined can rustle up a polished "product". The "product-without-process" had no place in the musical culture 50 years ago. It is not clear whether it is acceptable today. This, too, is perhaps only a matter of time. Once the present generation of cultural administrators retires, the inevitable will have to be accepted.

Some vestiges of traditional grooming still remain, and are producing fine vocalists committed to stylistic continuity and equipped for originality — how much longer, we cannot predict. The majority of practitioners of this individualistic art cannot, however, make a claim to stylistic originality.

The influential models of vocalism in the post-Independence era have been Amir Khan, Bhimsen Joshi, Kishori Amonkar, and Kumar Gandharva. These luminaries are thoroughbred products of gharana-grooming who have also been highly original interpreters of the tradition. They are great composers and also performers. But, their greatness has tempted subsequent generations to restrict their own roles to that of perfomers and to totally surrender to these luminaries the role of composers.

As a result, contemporary Khayal vocalism appears to be transforming an improvisation-dominant genre into a virtually pre-composed genre. Once the convergence of the roles of the composer and performer is jeopardised, there is little likelihood that thoroughbred originals of the calibre of Bhimsen Joshi, Amir Khan, Kishori Amonkar, and Kumar Gandharva will emerge on the scene in the foreseeable future. This constitutes some justification for connoisseurs to be anxious about the future of Khayal vocalism.

7

Thumree

Lost without Kathak

If you are witnessing a Kathak performance, the chances are that at least one of the items will be accompanied by a Thumree. The Thumree is a modern genre of semi-classical music, which originated as an accompaniment to the Kathak genre of north Indian dance, and evolved later as an independent art form. Its name is traced to "thumak" in Hindi, a phonetic suggestion of the graceful steps of a dancer with ankle bells. After seeing its days of glory in the courtesan districts of the eighteenth and nineteenth centuries, the musical genre finds itself eased out of the mainstream platform.

Kathak dance as well as the Thumree, evolved in the neighbourhood of Mathura, the birthplace of Lord Krishna. Thematically, both genres are immersed in the Bhakti movement, and the amorous joys of Radha and Krishna. The Thumree represents the stylisation of folk sources from the Brij (Mathura/Vrindavan) region by courtesans in response to the entertainment needs of a cultivated aristocracy. Benares and Lucknow were, till recently, the major centres of the Thumree art. Until the end of the nineteenth century, courtesans were the predominant

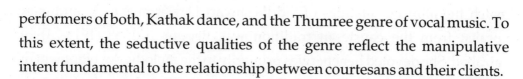

performers of both, Kathak dance, and the Thumree genre of vocal music. To this extent, the seductive qualities of the genre reflect the manipulative intent fundamental to the relationship between courtesans and their clients.

The genre subsumes two sub-genres — a brisk and lively form called the Bandish Thumree and a leisurely, sentimental form called Bol-banao Thumree. The latter is allied closely to Dadra, Chaiti, Kajri and other semi-classical forms, which are highly stylised versions of the folk music of the Benares region.

Ragas in Thumree

Though Thumrees are composed in ragas, the genre permits a libertarian approach to raga grammar. The melodic material for the genre is derived from a group of ragas, almost certainly of folk origin, which are typically "Thumree Ragas". These are: Dhani, Tilang, Shivranjani, Bhairavi, Khamaj, Piloo, Ghara, Zilla, Kafi, Pahari, Maanj Khamaj, Jhinjhoti, Desh, Tilak-Kamod, Mand, Kaushi-Dhani, Sindhura, Jangula and Bihari. A few of these ragas are also encountered in full-fledged classical treatment.

Tala in Thumree

Cutting through the maze of folk nomenclatures and multiple versions, and in contemporary language, the Bol-banao Thumree primarily uses Deepchandi of 14 beats, Keherva of eight beats, Dadra of six beats, and Tritala of 16 beats, rendered in a stylised, or probably folk, manner. These versions of Tritala are known by several names.

Landmark Personalities

Amongst the specialist performers of Thumree and the allied semi-classical genres, Siddheshwari Devi (1903-77) was, by far, the most outstanding in recent times. In the same generation, Rasoolan Bai (1902-74) came next in terms of stature. Badi Moti Bai (died: 1971), was another eminent Benares vocalist, whose Thumrees bespoke her solid classical training, but did not match the alluring qualities of Siddheshwari Devi's music. A landmark vocalist from the courtesan tradition was Begum Akhtar (1914-74) of Faizabad. She devoted her energies primarily to the melodic development of the Ghazal, and enriched its melodic content enough to bring it almost on par with the Bol-banao Thumree.

In the early twentieth century, the Bol-banao Thumree entered the mainstream, featuring usually as a tailpiece to a Khayal concert. Abdul Kareem Khan (1872-1936), the founder of the Kairana Gharana, virtually redefined the Thumree by taking the seductive out of the Benares Thumree, and replacing it with an intense poignancy and devotional fervour. In the generation after him, the Agra Gharana titan, Faiyyaz Khan (1886-1950) became immensely popular with his renditions of the Bol-banao Thumree. He also revived the Lucknow style of Bandish Thumree, and trained his foster son, Sharafat Hussain (1930-85), as a brilliant exponent of the genre. In the succeeding generation, the brothers from Patiala, Bade Ghulam Ali Khan (1903-68) and Barkat Ali Khan, revolutionised the Bol-banao genre. Bade Ghulam Ali's Thumrees were rich in

Siddheshwari Devi

ethnic flavours from his native Punjab and the neighbouring Rajasthan, Sindh, Kashmir and the North-West Frontier.

Other eminent Khayal singers who performed the Thumree with great élan in the first half of twentieth century were Vilayat Hussain Khan of Agra (1885-1962), Mushtaq Hussain (1878-1964) of Rampur-Sahaswan, Rehmat Khan of Gwalior (died: 1922), and Kesarbai Kerkar of Jaipur-Atrauli (1892-1977). However, none of them is credited with contributing significantly to

Abdul Kareem Khan

the distinctive identity of the genre. In fact, after Bade Ghulam Ali Khan, the Thumree renditions of Khayal singers have been increasingly criticised for not being sentimental enough.

Thumree in Instrumental Music

While being a poetry-dominant genre, the Thumree also represents a distinctive musical style. By adopting its musical elements, instrumental music has developed a "Thumree style", which is distinct from the Dhrupad and Khayal-inspired idioms.

The most significant instrumental exponent of the Thumree is obviously the Sarangi, which has been the standard accompaniment to the Thumree as well as the Khayal during the nineteenth century. Now frequently encountered as a soloist, a Sarangi player can do greater justice to a Thumree rendition than any other instrumentalist.

The Thumree and its allied semi-classical genres have also partially inspired the wind instruments. Its influence over Shehnai music is explained by Bismillah Khan, who belonged to Benares. Like the Shehnai, though to a lesser degree, the Bansuri (the bamboo flute), has conceded a significant place to the Thumree in its repertoire. This development is attributed to the phenomenal musicianship of two maestros, Pannalal Ghosh (1911-62) and Hariprasad Chaurasia (born: 1938).

Interestingly, even the plucked instruments succumbed to the charms of the Thumree. Their

Faiyyaz Khan

presence in this territory reached the highest level of sophistication in the hands of the Sitarist, Vilayat Khan, who succeeded in capturing the totality of the Thumree experience. Vilayat Khan's Thumree-inspired idiom has been imitated by host of Sitar and Sarod players not only from his own stylistic lineage but also of rival lineages.

The Thumree Today

By the early twentieth century, the brisk and lively Bandish Thumree had virtually merged with the Chhota Khayal. What still remained distinct in Thumree genre then was the leisurely Bol-banao Thumree, which was also fast losing its "tailpiece" position to the Bhajan and regional repertoire. The main reason for this could be its basic character as an art form. It was probably a unique product of the relationship between courtesans and their clients in the fertile soils irrigated by the Ganga and Yamuna during the eighteenth and nineteenth centuries. It was uncomfortable on the twentieth century concert platform, and hence withered away.

Girija Devi

At the time of this writing, the genre can claim only two vocalists of stature — Girija Devi (born: 1929), and Chhannulal Mishra — who are exclusively devoted to the practice of the Benares tradition of Thumree and its allied genres, such as Dadra, Chaiti, Kajri, etc. No worthy heirs to their mantle are yet visible on the horizon.

Amongst the leading Khayal exponents, Parveen Sultana (born: 1948) and Prabha Atre (born: 1932) are outstanding Bol-banao Thumree exponents. The Thumree, interestingly, appears to be experiencing a minor revival amongst male vocalists. Today's major vocalists, like Rashid Khan, Ulhas Kashalkar, and Ajoy Chakravarty perform Thumrees of both varieties with great attention to their intrinsic character. Female vocalists of the younger generation, especially from Maharashtra, have largely neglected the Thumree. This is important because, on the Khayal platform, ladies outnumber men several times over.

In its totality, the share of Thumree has shrunk drastically during the latter half of the twentieth century. While the poetry, melody and amorphous architecture of the Thumree may still have credible presenters, the mild and sustained inebriation characteristic of the genre is perhaps lost forever. With the complete concert of semi-classical music revolving around the Thumree having disappeared long ago, the Thumree appears to be faced with extinction.

The aesthetic space the Thumree occupied could not have disappeared with the eclipse of the genre. The space exists, and rival genres are attempting to fill it. The romanticist Khayal brigade — Kumar Gandharva, Kishori Amonkar, and Jasraj — has driven the Khayal closer to the emotional expressiveness of the Thumree. The other significant encroachment of the Thumree's space came from the Ghazal end, with Begum Akhtar and thereafter, Mehdi Hassan. They substantially widened the scope of melodic improvisation and raised the Ghazal to a level of sophistication approximating a Thumree.

The instrumental manifestations of Thumree aesthetics appear to be in good health. However, they seem to be independent of the health of the vocal genre. The vocal Thumree today appears as nearly extinct as Dhrupad did half a century ago. This is interesting. As Dhrupad itself proved, genres of music do not simply vanish. They go underground, reinvent themselves, and surface again to reclaim audiences. When conditions are favourable, the Thumree might have a better chance of doing so than Dhrupad did because it still remains active as a participant in the Kathak dance tradition, and unlike Dhrupad, it has not become dependent on foreign audiences.

8

The Tappa
The Camel Driver's Song

If you were driving a camel in the mountainous terrain of the North-West Frontier, and simultaneously trying to sing a brisk Khayal, what would you sound like? You would probably appear to be singing a Tappa.

The Tappa is a modern semi-classical genre of folk derivation, inspired by the songs of the camel drivers in Punjab and the NWFP bordering Afghanistan. The acceptance of the genre in genteel society by the late eighteenth century was synchronous with that of the Thumree. Unlike the Thumree, however, it achieved early acceptance amongst the Khayal lineages.

The refinement of the folk idiom into a stylised genre was accomplished by one Ghulam Nabi, who composed his Tappas under the pen-name "Shorie Miya". Ghulam Nabi's father, Ghulam Rasool, was an eminent Khayal vocalist in the employ of Nawab Asafuddaula (reign: 1775-97) of Awadh. Ghulam Nabi was trained in Khayal vocalism, but did not have a voice suitable for the genre. He travelled extensively in Punjab, mastered the Tappa idiom, and matured it enough to achieve distinction at the Awadh court upon his return.

Thereafter, the Tappa has had a trajectory similar to the Thumree. It struck roots in the courtesan districts of Lucknow and Benares, acquired a significant following in Bengal and eastern India probably through the tragic aesthete, Nawab Wajid Ali's entourage in exile, and also established itself as a companion to Khayal vocalism. In present times, though performances of the Tappa are none too frequent, the genre appears to have withstood the pressures of the Khayal-dominated environment better than the Thumree.

The Tappa Wave

Ghulam Nabi (Shorie Miya) trained several vocalists in the art of the Tappa. His father, who became a convert to this lively new genre, also taught the art to his students. As a result, the Tappa moved from its native Lucknow to Benares, Gwalior, and Calcutta, to become a part of the courtesan districts and the Khayal platform.

Amongst the Khayal lineages, Tappa received earliest acceptance from Gwalior. Natthan Peer Baksh (early nineteenth century), the founder of the Gwalior lineage, responded enthusiastically to the Tappa. Successive generations of Gwalior vocalists have thereafter preserved the Tappa art, and valued it as a means of cultivating exceptional vocal agility. In the first quarter of the twentieth century, Gwalior vocalists worked closely with musicologist, V.N. Bhatkhande, to document Tappa songs, thus contributing to the stature of the genre and also its survival.

Although other Khayal lineages did not adopt the Tappa as enthusiastically as did Gwalior, Tappa flavours had begun to infiltrate Khayal vocalism by the early twentieth century. Glimpses of this influence can be seen in the music of Faiyyaz Khan and later, Bade Ghulam Ali Khan.

According to Rohit Desai, a leading archivist and music historian, approximately 100 Tappa recordings were published on 78 rpm discs during the twentieth century. In a limited discography published by him, the overwhelming majority of the named singers are specialist singers of the semi-classical genres. The list includes only a handful of Khayal singers, mainly from Gwalior, Agra, and Rampur-Sahaswan Gharanas.

Salient Stylistic Features

The identifying feature of the Tappa is a mischievous treatment of melody. The melody is not only naughty within itself, but also rhythmically clever. The bouncy ethnicity of Tappa melody has often been compared to a ride on the back of a camel — a slightly far-fetched metaphor. A Tappa is so distinct a musical experience that it is easy to identify with minimal familiarity, but difficult to describe. As a starting point for the entirely unfamiliar, a Tappa may be described as an impish rendition of a Chhota (brisk) Khayal, but considerably more puckish than a Bandish Thumree.

Tappas are composed mainly in "Thumree ragas", such as Bhairavi, Khamaj, Desh, Kafi, Jhinjhoti, Piloo, and Barwa. They are generally set to variants of the 16-beat Tritala. A few Tappas have also been composed in Ektala of 12 beats. In either tala, Tappas are sung in medium tempo, so that the melodic and rhythmic playfulness of the genre is effectively communicated. The lyrics are mostly in Punjabi or Sindhi, or the languages of the North-West Frontier. Compositions bearing the Shorie Miya signature are still the most popular, though the genre has benefited from the contributions of several composers thereafter.

Although the Tappa apparently relied on the Bandish Thumree and the Chhota Khayal for its format, it has, in turn, influenced the Khayal genre by giving birth to a hybrid form, the Tap-Khayal. This form is normally rendered in the "classical" ragas, but has the distinct vivacity of the Tappa in its treatment of melody. Tap-Khayals enjoy considerable stature because of their demanding aesthetics, and are performed in several gharanas of Khayal vocalism.

The Tappa Today

The presence of the Tappa on the contemporary concert platform is slightly better than that of the Thumree. While their relegation to the background may have some common features and causes, the Tappa can be viewed individually.

The major repository of Tappa musicianship was the courtesan tradition of Benares, which specialised in the semi-classical genres such as the Thumree, along with the allied folk-based genres of the region. This tradition was a unique product of its environment, and has been speeding towards extinction, taking the Tappa along with it.

Malini Rajurkar

The other significant repository of Tappa musicianship is the Gwalior Khayal Gharana. From the second quarter of the twentieth century, several Gwalior vocalists drifted towards the vocalism of the Agra Gharana in an attempt to reinvent their stylistic legacy. One of the results of the Gwalior-Agra confluence was the gradual disappearance of the Tappa from Gwalior repertoire. Traditional Gwalior vocalism has been increasingly marginalised after the departure of D.V. Paluskar and Omkarnath Thakur (neither of them sang Tappas). The Khayal gharanas, which gained ascendancy in the post-Independence era — primarily Kairana and Jaipur-Atrauli — ignored the Tappa in favour of either the Thumree or Bhajans. Bengal, once an important Tappa centre, is yet to produce front-ranking vocalists with a serious interest in the Tappa.

On the contemporary platform, the Tappa appears — when it does — primarily as a tailpiece to a Khayal rendition, and as an alternative to a Thumree. The dominance of the Khayal platform by vocalists from Maharashtra has caused this role to be handed over to Bhajans (devotional songs) and Natya Sangeet (Raga-based music from the regional theatre). One of the keys to this phenomenon, though a minor one, may be that Tappa lyrics are written mainly in Punjabi, Sindhi or Pushto, languages understood by even fewer people than Braja-Bhasha, the language of the Thumree and the Khayal.

Manjiri Asnare-Kelkar

Despite its limitations, several features of the Tappa suggest a better chance for its survival than that of the Thumree. Because of its excessively mischievous treatment of melody, Khayal, the dominant mainstream genre, cannot encroach upon the Tappa's territory as easily as it could upon the Thumree. Nor can the poetry-dominant genres like the Ghazal compete for its aesthetic space from the other end. The revival of the genre, therefore, depends more on the interest of musicians and the acceptance of the genre by contemporary audiences. Indicators of these factors deserve attention.

The contemporary scene can claim the towering presence of Girija Devi (born: 1929), as the only specialist of the semi-classical genres who excels at Tappa rendition. Amongst established Khayal vocalists, the significant Tappa exponents are Laxman Krishnarao Pandit (born: 1932) and Malini Rajurkar (born: 1941). This picture would look dismal. But if we look for a ray of hope, Manjiri Asnare-Kelkar (born: 1971), a successful Khayal vocalist, is reviving a constituency for the Tappa.

Her induction into the genre is interesting. Manjiri had her initial training in the Gwalior tradition. Early in her grooming, she became an admirer of Malini Rajurkar, especially of her Tappa renderings. She acquired all available Tappa recordings of Malini, painstakingly took down notations, verified lyrics with published sources, and started performing them with great success (interview with the author on 5 May 2003). She later became a disciple of Madhusudan Kanetkar, the Jaipur-Atrauli Gharana stalwart, who studied the Tappa specially to be able to help her organise and polish her renditions.

These may be unorthodox and rare conditions for the continuity of a genre. But, Manjiri's success with the Tappa confirms several promising features of the genre. Most of all, it establishes the possibility of acquiring respectable proficiency without expert supervision, and the genre's potential for broad-spectrum audience appeal. These factors justify greater optimism for the Tappa than for the Thumree.

9

The Rudra Veena
Headed for the Museum

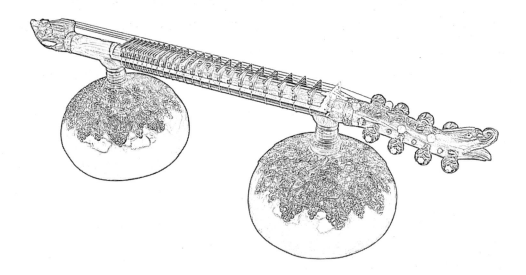

Jn the early years after Independence, the Dhrupad genre was frequently described as "a museum piece". This description was more appropriate to the Rudra Veena (commonly called the Been), than to the vocal art. Half a century later, the vocal art is showing signs of survival, while the art of the Been appears truly headed for the museum.

The Been is an instrument of entirely Indian origin. It is revered because of its association with Rudra (Lord Shiva), the Originator of the performing arts. Shiva is believed to have created the instrument, inspired by the reclining figure of his Divine Consort, Parvati. Historically, however, the instrument appears to have evolved from the Laghu Kinnari Veena in the 12th or 13th centuries. The instrument is thus a product of the middle ages, falsifying the frequent description of the instrument as "ancient".

From Centre-Stage to the Brink

Been music is inseparably linked to the Dhrupad genre of art music, which saw its days of glory between the fifteenth and eighteenth centuries. The Been originally accompanied vocal Dhrupad recitals; the content of their music thus came to be identical in melodic and rhythmic respects. But the two arts also evolved their independent performing domains.

During the reign of the Mughal Emperor, Akbar (sixteenth century), Miya Tansen's children perpetuated the art of the Been, and also adapted it to the Rabab, the forerunner of the Sarod. A couple of centuries later, during the reign of Emperor Mohammad Shah "Rangile" (reign: 1719-48), eminent Been players developed the idiom of the Sitar. Thus, the legacy of the Been emerged as the fountainhead of both the major modern plucked lutes — Sarod and Sitar.

Dhrupad and the Been started losing ground by the late eighteenth century when the decaying Mughal Empire prompted leading musicians to drift away from Delhi and its neighbourhood in search of alternative patronage. This exposed them to diverse stylistic influences, many of which were already being swept by the achievements of the rival Khayal, Thumree and Tappa genres.

The post-Dhrupad environment began to make a different set of stylistic demands on the art of the plucked instruments. By its very design, the Been

was unsuited for fulfilling these demands. The Sitar was filling the vacuum, but was not yet acoustically sophisticated enough to challenge the Been, especially in the leisurely rendition of the alap.

To compete effectively with the Been, sitarists devised the Surbahar (around 1825), an instrument which combined the acoustic richness of the Been with a playing technique akin to the Sitar. This led to the practice of sitarists playing the Been style alap on the Surbahar followed by post-Dhrupad music on the Sitar. As a solo instrument, the Been ultimately succumbed to this challenge. Simultaneously, the decline of Dhrupad vocalism was also shrinking the Been's presence as an accompanist.

Starting from the mid-nineteenth century, a majority of the lineages of Dhrupad music diverted their energies to the Khayal genre. Synchronously, Been practitioners were forced to make a living by teaching music to sitarists, Surbahar players, and sarodists. The decline of the Been was dramatic after Independence which dispossessed the feudal aristocracy, a part of which had continued to support Dhrupad and the Been even in its sunset years.

The Been got a breather once Western Europe warmed up to Dhrupad in the mid-1960s. By the 1980s, after the vocal Dhrupad genre had acquired an enthusiastic following abroad, the market for the Been was cultivated by Asad Ali Khan, and Zia Mohiuddin Dagar. Both performed extensively in Europe and the US, and broke the traditional

Zia Mohiuddin Dagar

barrier to teaching the art beyond ties of kinship. They accepted European and American students and seeded a self-propagating constituency for the

Been in the West. Dhrupad thus became a unique phenomenon in art music —losing ground at home and flourishing amongst aliens.

At the time of writing, the vocal art of Dhrupad boasts of a small group of dedicated vocalists who are credible musicians at home, but dependent largely on the Western market for their livelihood. The number of Been players is much smaller than vocalists, and they could well be more dependent on foreign audiences than the vocalists.

Interesting Design Aspects

The Been is an interesting example of the re-engineering of an instrument to suit changing conditions. Essentially, it is an instrument of simple construction with a tubular stem acting as the column resonator, and two large dried gourds attached towards its two ends functioning as chamber resonators.

The Been is the only Indian instrument which is tailor-made for the musician, like an upper garment. This is because the two gourds have to be

Shamsuddin Faridi

fitted just right to give him a proper grip, withstand the stress of him virtually wrestling with it, and also leave enough room for him to breathe comfortably.

Traditionally, the stem was made of bamboo, which tended to split in a couple of years. Re-fastening the gourds to a new stem was a highly skilled task. Bamboo was later replaced with shisham wood, which lasted six to eight years. Stems are now made from teakwood, which has a useful life of twenty years. Incidentally, wooden stems also deliver a more microphone friendly sound than bamboo stems.

Once the wooden stem was developed, it could be equipped with multiple sockets for detachable gourds. The musician can now screw in the gourds according to his dimensions and convenience. This innovation has removed the necessity of having a tailor-made instrument. Incidentally, this has also made the instrument eminently portable — a great advantage considering that today's Been players are much busier abroad than in India.

The Disappearing Breed

Based on a survey of historical works, it appears that there were 24 significant Beenkars in the nineteenth century. This is more likely to reflect the poverty of documentation, than of the profession. The history of the Been in the twentieth century is probably more reliable. The first half of the century saw the departure of 21 significant Beenkars. In the latter half of the

twentieth century, 10 significant Beenkars departed from the scene. The first eight months of 2011 saw the departure of two eminent Beenkars — Asad Ali Khan, and Shamsuddin Faridi.

Asad Ali Khan

The survey reveals an amazing variety of profiles amongst Been practitioners. For one, it includes Hindus and Moslems, each in substantial numbers. Secondly, it covers almost all parts of non-peninsular India. Thirdly, it includes professional musicians, priests, monks, aristocrats, royalty, and even courtesans. And, finally, it includes Beenkars who founded great lineages of Khayal vocalism, as also those who taught great Sitar, Surbahar and Sarod players. This variety reflects the all-pervasive presence of the Been in Hindustani music before it relinquished it in favour of instruments capable of greater melodic and rhythmic agility.

At the time of writing, and on reasonable reckoning, there are only four living Beenkars in India with training in a well-established lineage of Been music — Pandharinath Kolhapure, the son of Krishnarao Kolhapure; Hindaraj Diwekar, the son of Shivrambuwa Diwekar; and Bahauddin Dagar, the son of Zia Mohiuddin Dagar. In recent times, Jyoti Hegde of Dharwad, a disciple of the late Beenkar, Bindumadhav Pathak, has attracted considerable attention. Only the last three named here belong the post-Independence generation. In the last quarter of the twentieth century, a few European students of the Been achieved a respectable level of competence. Amongst them is Philippe Bruguiere, a respected scholar.

Been Music Today

By the mid-twentieth century, Been practitioners had already started losing their moorings in its traditional aesthetic space — the Dhrupad genre — without quite having found an anchor in the contemporary. If any art form is to evolve in terms of richness, its performers need relevant reference points within the musical culture. To this extent, the Been could be faced with two daunting realities.

Firstly, vocal Dhrupad music, which constituted the reference point for the Been, is no longer represented by a sizeable pool of quality musicianship. Therefore, the traditional ideation resource of the Beenkar is shrinking speedily. At the same time, its ability to absorb post-Dhrupad musical values also remains unproven. Secondly, the number of Dhrupad musicians pursuing the instrumental art of the Been is very small, and the numbers are shrinking fast. Very soon, the remaining Beenkars will have virtually no contemporary left against whom to benchmark their musicianship. These are, regrettably, not conditions in which an art can be expected to flourish.

The distinguished Beenkar, Asad Ali Khan (died: 2011), foresaw extinction for the Been art unless job opportunities were created in India for

its practitioners (interview with Utpal Banerjee, Sruti, October 2002). This is a debatable proposition.

The cultural process is constantly pulling some instruments upwards, and pushing others downwards, in terms of popularity and stature. It has never been easy to ascertain which of the two forces — the size and quality of the supply or the size of the demand — causes the spiral to change direction for any particular instrument. For this reason, protectionist interventions of this kind have not worked in the past, and could fail again.

10

The Sitar
From Nowhere to Everywhere
in 300 Years

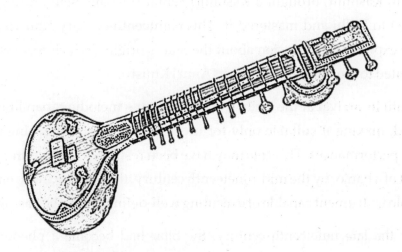

HE post-Independence era has been the Golden Age of instrumental music in the Hindustani tradition. Substantial credit for this goes to the Sitar and to sitarists. The instrument entered the mainstream as an heir to the medieval Rudra Veena to later become its rival, and finally, its survivor. Its journey to the pinnacle of instrumental music has taken about 300 years.

The Sitar is a long-necked fretted lute of the plucked variety. This family of instruments is believed to have come to India from Central Asia. The most popular theory attributes its "invention" to Amir Khusro (1253/1234-1355), an influential mystic, poet, and musician, who served the court of Alauddin Khalji (1296-1316). This theory has few takers now. Though Sitar-like instruments have probably existed in different parts of the country even before Amir Khusro's times, the Sitar is now accepted as being a recent development.

The first mention of the Sitar (1739) names a Khusro Khan, most likely, a brother of the legendary Niamat Khan (Sadarang) in the court of Emperor Mohammad Shah "Rangile" (reign: 1719-48). This Khusro Khan spent some years in Kashmir, brought a Kashmiri Sehtar (Persian: Seh = three + tar = strings) to Delhi and mastered it. This eighteenth-century Khusro (Khan) might explain the confusion about the Sitar's origins, which were wrongly attributed to the thirteenth century (Amir) Khusro.

Until its arrival at the Delhi Court, the Sitar's melodic capabilities were limited, making it suitable only for orchestration supporting singing and dance performances. This role may have been restricted to strumming, akin to that of a banjo. By the mid-nineteenth century, the Sitar had, also emerged as a solo instrument capable of executing well-defined melodic passages.

By the late nineteenth century, the Sitar had become a phenomenon, attracting a large number of professional and amateur musicians in various parts of the country, and acquiring a place in the Courts of princes. Musicians from Rudra Veena playing families were forced to shed their elitism, and start performing on the Sitar, and also start teaching it. The instrument had developed an idiom of its own, inspired initially by the Rudra Veena, but responding progressively to changing aesthetic values.

These developments were obviously accompanied by changes in the design and construction of the instrument — a process that has continued in later years as musicians have wanted the instrument to deliver music of progressively greater sophistication.

Compositional Styles in Sitar Music

The earliest compositional style specifically for sitar was evolved in mid-eighteenth century by Firoz Khan, either the son or nephew of Khusro Khan. Probably because of the difficulty of executing them on the long-necked Sitar, Firoz Khani compositions found greater favour with performers on the short-necked Rabab (the ancestor of the Sarod). Firoz Khani compositions are no longer heard on the Sitar, but remain a part of the Sarod repertoire.

In the early nineteenth century, Firoz Khan's son, Masit Khan, composed stroke-formats for the Sitar in all the major talas. But, his stroke-format for Tritala turned out to be most popular. The Masit Khani format in Tritala is, till today, the standard slow-tempo format for Sitar as well as Sarod compositions.

The next most significant stroke pattern for Sitar compositions was created by Ghulam Raza Khan of Lucknow in the early nineteenth century during the reign of Nawab Wajid Ali Shah of Awadh. The Raza Khani format remains, to this day, an important part of a sitarist's repertoire. Ghulam Raza's inspiration for his medium-to-fast tempo compositions in Tritala came from the cadences of the lively Bandish-ki-Thumree genre of vocal music, performed as accompaniment to Kathak dance.

In the early years, the Masit Khani and Raza Khani stroke-based formats were dominant because the Sitar was still an unrefined acoustic machine, requiring high-frequency plucking. Once the re-engineering of the instrument began, the lure of vocalism began to assert itself. The flourishing post-Dhrupad vocal genres — mainly Khayal, and Thumree — steadily drew Sitar music towards a more leisurely and ornate treatment of melody.

The re-engineering gathered momentum in the early part of the twentieth century, encouraged greatly by the emerging acoustic

environment. The arrival of the microphone and recording technologies enabled the faithful delivery of the finest nuances in musical expression, thus encouraging sitarists to seek a wider variety of stylistic options. As a result, the Sitar today renders compositions of various melodic and rhythmic personalities.

Talas in Sitar Music

Although early sitar music was performed in a variety of talas, performers soon gravitated towards Tritala (16 beats), which has remained its primary tala up to the present. A diversification of temporal orientations has taken place in the latter half of the twentieth century. As a result, a fair amount of sitar music is now performed in other talas — mainly Jhaptala (10 beats) and Rupak (7 beats), but occasionally also Ektala (12 beats), Deepchandi (14 beats) and Dhamar (14 beats).

Stylistic Lineages of Sitar Music

Vilayat Khan

The notion of a gharana is not as well defined in Sitar music as it is, say, in Khayal vocalism. However, distinctive stylistic lineages identified in 1990 at the ITC-SRA Seminar on the Sitar suggest the various claims to distinctiveness. These were:

(a) The Maihar Gharana (also called the "Maihar Senia" Gharana): Maihar is the town in Madhya Pradesh, which its founder, Allauddin Khan, had made his home. The "Senia" suffix links the lineage to Wazir Khan of Rampur, who was a descendant of the legendary Miya Tansen at the court of emperor Akbar. The foremost sitarist of this lineage is Ravi Shankar.

(b)   The Etawah Gharana (also called the Imdad Khani Gharana): This lineage is identified with Etawah in Uttar Pradesh, which was the original home of Imdad Khan, its fountainhead. At the turn of the twentieth century, the foremost exponent of the gharana's style was Vilayat Khan (died: 2004).

(c)   The Jaipur Beenkar/Sitar Gharana: This is a lineage of Rudra Veena players from Jaipur, who evolved and propagated a Rudra Veena-based style of sitar playing. The last significant performer in this tradition was Bimal Mukherjee (1930-96).

(d)   The Bishnupur Gharana: This nomenclature refers to the town of Bishnupur in Bengal, which emerged as a major centre of music in the latter half of the nineteenth century. The most distinguished exponent of this lineage is Manilal Nag.

(e)   The Indore Gharana: This is a lineage of Rudra Veena players, sitarists, and vocalists who had settled in the erstwhile principalities of Indore, Dewas, Jawra, and Jabalpore in Madhya Pradesh. The most significant contemporary Sitarist of this tradition is Abdul Halim Jaffar Khan.

(f)   The Senia Gharana: The term "Senia" applies to the descendants of the legendary Miya Tansen. Of the various Senia streams of Sitar music, the only one active at the turn of the century was the one hailing from Benares. The last distinguished performer of this style was Mushtaque Ali Khan. His important present-day disciples are Debabrata Choudhary and Netai Bose.

(g)   The Lucknow Gharana: The Lucknow Gharana is essentially a lineage of Sarod players. But, it has also produced distinguished Sitar players such as Ilyas Khan (1924-89), Waliullah Khan (1890-1951) and Yusuf Ali Khan (1877-1962). By the end of the twentieth century, the gharana reported no significant musicianship.

Sitar Styles Today

Amongst the major instruments, the Sitar has been singularly fortunate in producing two giants in the same generation — Vilayat Khan (Etawah) and Ravi Shankar (Maihar) — who created distinct, and almost rival, musical worlds around themselves. They even developed their own distinctive designs for the Sitar. As a result, music shops now offer you a choice between a "Ravi Shankar Style Sitar" and a "Vilayat Khan Style Sitar". Even sitarists groomed in other gharanas have gravitated towards one of the two styles. Though seven gharanas of Sitar music were identified only in 1990, several of them are already devoid of a significant presence on the concert platform.

The future of stylistic diversity is uncertain. The strength of homogenising forces is already evident in the fact that the Vilayat Khan style is proliferating much faster amongst professional sitarists than the Ravi Shankar style. The cultural environment, too, is not particularly conducive to the flowering of sharply differentiated styles.

Ravi Shankar

A market of subcontinental, and even global, dimensions appears to reward music conforming to the dominant models. As a result, Sitar music of the foreseeable future could be stylistically less — rather than more — diverse than it is at present.

11

The Surbahar
In Search of an Indian Bach

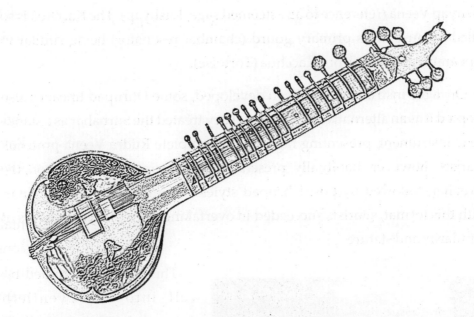

You may have seen and heard it. But, maybe, you have not. It looks like a giant Sitar, and sounds like the Rudra Veena. In terms of its design, the Surbahar is to the Sitar, what the Cello is to the Violin. And, the parallels do not end here. Read on.

The Surbahar was developed around CE 1825, by Ghulam Mohammad, a prominent sitarist in the Awadh principality (Lucknow). He was also an expert craftsman.

Because the Sitar was not, at that stage a sufficiently sophisticated acoustic machine, it could not deliver the Rudra Veena style alap (leisurely prelude, unaccompanied by percussion). Ghulam Mohammad felt the need to devise an instrument which combined the handling convenience of the Sitar with the melodic potential and acoustic richness of the Rudra Veena.

The instrument Ghulam Mohammad designed was, however, not entirely new in its basic design concept. It is a modified version of a Kacchua Sitar, also known as the Kachhapi Veena (Kachhap= Sanskrit for Tortoise) or Kashyap Veena (reference to an esteemed sage, Kashyap). The Kacchua is so called because of its primary gourd (chamber resonator) being similar in appearance to the shell of a Kacchua (Tortoise).

Once the instrument had been developed, some Dhrupad lineages also adopted it as an alternative to the Been. They treated the Surbahar as a stand-alone instrument, presenting ragas in the complete Rudra Veena protocol. Sitarists, however, habitually presented the Dhrupad style alap on the Surbahar, followed by post-Dhrupad styles of compositions on the Sitar. With this format, sitarists succeeded in overtaking Been players in terms of popularity and stature.

Enayet Khan

This pattern continued till well into the twentieth century. As the Sitar itself evolved technically and stylistically, it took over the elaborate Rudra Veena alap, and even enhanced its sophistication. Consequently, during the latter half of the twentieth century, with the Dhrupad genre also being in a

state of decline, the Surbahar suffered a steady depletion in the number of performers.

The contemporary Sitar of enhanced musical capability now threatens the Surbahar with extinction. This is understandable because, though they look similar, the Sitar and Surbahar are very different instruments, with the Surbahar also being physically much more demanding. The additional effort of mastering two instruments was acceptable when the Sitar was relatively handicapped. Design improvements on the Sitar made a twin-instrument format unnecessary and unattractive.

Though its time may now be running out, the Surbahar remains a major link of continuity between the Dhrupad and post-Dhrupad styles of instrumental music. The instrument is still being performed by musicians around 50, who respect its traditional role. But, credible Surbahar players below 50 are impossible to find.

Musicianship

The originator, Ghulam Mohammad's family, played a pioneering role in the propagation of the Surbahar. In this, it was greatly supported by the landed aristocracy of Bengal, particularly the famous Tagore family. Another beneficiary of this patronage was the distinguished Sitarist, Imdad Khan. He had studied the Rudra Veena under the famous Indore-based Beenkar, Bande Ali Khan, and emerged as an equally formidable performer on the Surbahar.

In later years, the lineage of Imdad Khan perpetuated the art and practises it till today.

Up to the middle of the twentieth century, three other lineages persisted with the art of the Surbahar. Allauddin Khan, founder of the Maihar Gharana, trained his daughter, Annapoorna Devi on the Surbahar. In her early years in the profession, she performed solo as well as duets with Ravi

Shankar. She retired from the profession in the 1950s, and devoted her remaining life to teaching. The other leading Surbahar player of the era was Mushtaque Ali Khan. The Rudra Veena maestro, Zia Mohiuddin Dagar, trained some students on the Surbahar. However, none of these mentors appear to have found heirs for their prowess with the Surbahar.

Surbahar in the Imdad Khan Lineage

In the Imdad Khan lineage (also known as the Etawah Gharana) the Surbahar has been an essential part of the training of its members, irrespective of whether they performed on the Sitar or the Surbahar.

Sahebdad Khan, Vilayat Khan's great grandfather, was so competent a Surbahar exponent, that many believed that it was he who invented it. His son, Imdad Khan, was a formidable Surbahar and Sitar player, as were his two sons, Enayet Khan (Vilayat Khan's father) and Waheed Khan (Vilayat Khan's uncle). Starting from Imdad Khan, recordings exist by way of evidence of the contribution of this lineage to the art of the Surbahar.

Imrat Khan

Vilayat Khan, and his brother, Imrat Khan, both received training on the Surbahar from their uncle, Waheed Khan. At some stage, Vilayat Khan ceded the Surbahar territory to Imrat Khan, and decided to concentrate on the Sitar. This bifurcation of territories has been most rewarding for the brothers and for the world of music in general. On rare occasions, however, Vilayat Khan did perform on the Surbahar, and his recordings are available.

In the Imdad Khan lineage, the Surbahar technique has now achieved a melodic continuity comparable to a fretless instrument, this being the primary intention of its design and technique. The three-tiered alap-jod-jhala derived from the Rudra Veena idiom has remained the basic idiom of the Surbahar; but Dhrupad stylistics have progressively yielded to an influence of Khayal-oriented treatment of melody.

The Surbahar as a Duet Instrument

Surbahar-Sitar duets began soon after the Surbahar was developed. This format fell into disuse, until its revival around the middle of the twentieth century, when Annapoorna Devi and Ravi Shankar briefly performed duets. In the mid-1960s, came the first major attempt at reviving the duet format.

The second revival began with the recording of a duet (A Night at the Taj: EMI: EALP: 1323) with Vilayat Khan playing the Sitar and Imrat Khan, the Surbahar. This recording encouraged the notion of the Surbahar as a male voice and the Sitar as a female voice. It also enabled the Surbahar, more categorically now than ever before, to break into percussion-accompanied presentation of post-Dhrupad compositions. This was followed by more duets of Vilayat Khan, not merely with his brother, Imrat Khan (EMI: ASD: 4980), but also his son, Shujaat Khan on the Surbahar (Navras: NRCC: 0533).

The Surbahar Today

Its recent achievements notwithstanding, a question mark hangs over the future of the instrument. The art of the Surbahar as a solo instrument is being seriously pursued today only by two musicians — Imrat Khan, and his son, Irshad Khan. However, even their appearances are far more frequent as Sitarists than as Surbahar players.

Because of its unique depth and seriousness, the Surbahar has a valuable role to play in duets with the Sitar or other instruments. But, performing duets cannot be a full-time profession in Hindustani music. With super-

human effort, sitarists have been able to take Surbahar music into the agility of Sitar territory. But, this too does not help, because the Sitar can now do everything the Surbahar can do. We are then left with only the unique sound of the Surbahar as its raison d'etre. This alone cannot reshape the Surbahar's destiny. So, we come back to the proposition that the survival of the Surbahar could require sitarists to master two different instruments.

Quite independently of this hurdle, contemporary conditions do not appear particularly friendly to the Surbahar. Hindustani music today services a global audience, and requires musicians to travel constantly within India and abroad. Unlike the Sitar, which is portable, the Surbahar is an unwieldy instrument. The Rudra Veena had a similar problem, which its craftsmen solved rather cleverly by introducing detachable gourds. The Surbahar does not lend itself to a similar solution because of its construction.

In order to continue drawing audiences and attracting talent, the Surbahar needs to define a unique solo idiom for itself. In Western music, the cello once faced a similar situation. Neither its role in orchestration, nor its encroachment upon violin territory, could unlock its musical potential. This happened only when composers like Bach and Boccherini started writing music especially for the instrument.

12

The Sarod
The Meteoric Rise

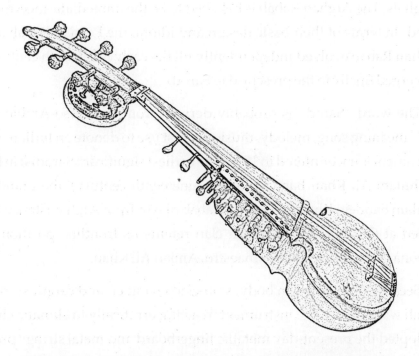

The Sarod, the instrument of Ali Akbar Khan and Amjad Ali Khan, is today a rival of the Sitar for popularity and stature. Its maturity conceals the fact that its transformation from a crude acoustic machine into a scintillating musical instrument has taken place largely in the twentieth century.

Instruments of the Sarod family are known to have been played in India around CE 600, perhaps even earlier.

However, the Sarod's identifiable ancestors apparently came from the Middle East. The instrument has two ancestors, both called Rabab.

The first Rabab came to India from Persia in the eleventh century along with the Gazhnavid occupation of the Punjab. In the sixteenth century, Akbar's court gave it a prominent place along with the Rudra Veena. Before Akbar's time, however, the Afghan Rabab, different in design from the Persian Rabab, had entered India with Pathan soldiers serving the early Mughals. The Afghan Rabab is believed to be the immediate ancestor of the Sarod. In terms of their basic design and idiom, the Persian Rabab and the Afghan Rabab evolved independently till the early nineteenth century, and converged finally in the present-day Sarod.

The word "Sarod" is probably derived from the Perso-Arabic "Shah-rud", meaning song, melody, music. Its first use to denote an Indian musical instrument is encountered in 1830. The earliest significant Sarodist in history is Ghulam Ali Khan Bangash (early nineteenth century), the grandson of Ghulam Bandegi Khan Bangash, a Rabab player from Afghanistan, who had settled at Gwalior. The Bangash clan retains its frontline position in the persona of the contemporary maestro, Amjad Ali Khan.

Because of its wooden body, skin-clad chamber, and catgut strings, the Rabab was an unstable instrument, reacting erratically to climatic changes. It adopted the present-day metallic fingerboard and metal strings probably from the Sursingar, a magnified variant of the Rabab, which is now extinct. With this change, the Sarod became the only plucked instrument in Hindustani music to have a shell made of wood, and an upper made of skin and metal, thus defining its unique acoustics.

Considerable re-engineering of the Sarod took place during the 1930s to make it the sophisticated instrument we hear today. This re-engineering is attributed to the legendary Guru, Allauddin Khan, and his brother, Ayet Ali Khan, who was a Surbahar exponent and also an expert craftsman. Though

their design may have become something of an "industry standard", alternative designs also have a distinguished following.

With constant re-engineering and exceptional musicianship enlarging the scope of melody, the martial history of the Afghan Rabab, and the robust aural experience are no longer dominant in Sarod music. But, they remain integral to the Sarod's musical personality.

Compositional Styles

The compositions of Firoz Khan, the mid-eighteenth century sitarist, who first introduced Rabab players to mainstream Hindustani music, failed to enthuse sitarists, but were eagerly adopted by Rabab players, and later Sarod players. Feroze Khani compositions in medium tempo remain, to this day, a part of an accomplished sarodist's repertoire. From the sitarist's repertoire, the Sarod also adopted the Masit Khani and Raza Khani formats for slow-tempo and fast-tempo Tritala compositions respectively. These two compositional formats are, today, as integral to Sarod music, as they are to Sitar music.

The legacy of traditional Rabab compositions constitutes the specialist territory of the Sarod. Their approaches to rhythm as well as melody are uniquely suited to the acoustic and mechanical aspects of the instrument.

In the post-Independence period, the influence of vocalism started making itself felt in Sarod music. This path was shown by Vilayat Khan, who exploited the enhanced melodic capabilities of his own re-engineered Sitar to launch a breathtakingly fresh vocalised idiom. Under his influence, Sarod players began to adapt Khayal, Tarana, and Thumree compositions for rendition on their instruments.

The compositional styles evident in contemporary Sarod music have thus come to reflect almost the entire spectrum of musical attitudes and orientations encountered in Hindustani music since medieval times.

Talas in Sarod Music

The robust Sarod idiom has traditionally had a bias in favour of the rhythmic element. The instrument, therefore, expresses itself in a wider range of talas than any other contemporary instrument. The instrument acquired its considerable dependence on Tritala (16 beats), from the Sitar, and inherited the Rabab legacy of compositions in a variety of talas — mainly Rupak (7 beats), Jhaptala (10 beats), and Dhamar (14 beats). In fact, Ali Akbar Khan went much farther, and performed even in talas of 6½, 9½ and 11½ beats, created by him. In recent years, primarily under his influence, several Sarod players and sitarists of the younger generation have also adopted such mind-bender patterns for their renditions.

Stylistic Legacies in Sarod Music

Ali Akbar Khan

Despite the obvious limitations of stylistic specialisation with reference to so young an instrument, certain lineages of Rabab/Sarod players have claimed distinctive status. The most authoritative recent identification of these lineages was done in 1991 at a Seminar conducted by the ITC Sangeet Research Academy. The seminar identified five lineages that have been represented by quality musicianship in the post-Independence period.

   (a)   The Maihar lineage, also sometimes referred to as the Maihar-Seniya lineage: The lineage is named after the town of Maihar in Madhya Pradesh, which Allauddin Khan, its founder, made his home. The Seniya suffix refers to the founder's principal Guru, Wazir Khan of Rampur, a descendant of Miya Tansen. After the demise of Ali Akbar

Khan in 2009, this lineage is represented by his son, Ashish Khan, and a large number of Indian and foreign disciples.

(b)   The lineage of Mohammad Amir Khan: The founder of the lineage, Mohammad Amir Khan was 6th generation descendant of Ghulam Ali Khan Bangash, the first Sarod player on record. Through his distinguished disciple, Radhika Mohan Maitra, this lineage has conserved the traditional Rabab idiom as the primary idiom of the Sarod. In recent times, this lineage has been represented by Maitra's disciples, Buddhadev Dasgupta and Kalyan Mukherjea.

(c)   The lineage of Ghulam Bandegi Khan Bangash: This lineage traces its origins to Ghulam Bandegi Khan Bangash, the grandfather of Ghulam Ali Khan Bangash, the first Sarod player on record. On the contemporary concert platform, this lineage is represented by Amjad Ali Khan.

(d)   The Lucknow-Shahjehanpur lineage: This lineage traces its origins to Najaf Ali Khan (1705-60) of Shahjehanpur and Madar Khan (1704-52) of Lucknow. Theirs was a lineage of Afghan Rabab players, groomed in the Dhrupad/Rudra Veena idiom. The last significant Sarod player of this lineage was Sakhawat Hussain Khan (1875-1955) who served on the faculty of the Bhatkhande Music University in Lucknow.

(e)   The Niamatullah-Karamatulla Khan lineage: Niamatullah Khan was an Afghan Rabab player, who moved to Calcutta from Awadh in 1857 along with Nawab Wajid Ali Shah in exile. Niamatullah and his son, Karamatulla established a lineage of Rabab, Sursingar and Sarod players. Karamatullah Khan's son, Ishtiaque Ahmed, was also an outstanding Sarod player. The last significant exponent of this lineage was Shyam Ganguly.

Sarod Styles Today

The contemporary Sarod idiom reflects three principal tendencies. The traditional Rabab-influenced idiom dominates the music of the lineage of

Amjad Ali Khan

Mohammad Amir Khan, represented by the disciples of Radhika Mohan Maitra. The Rudra Veena-influenced idiom, incorporating several other influences, dominates the music of the Maihar Seniya stylistic lineage — Allauddin Khan, and his son, Ali Akbar Khan. In the lineage of Ghulam Ali Khan Bangash, his direct descendant, Amjad Ali Khan is credited with driving the instrument's idiom towards modern vocalism.

Considering the recency of the Sarod's emergence as a front ranking instrument, and Ali Akbar Khan's towering presence over it, most music lovers may not discern the stylistic variety on display today. But, it does exist, and is being reinforced by systematic propagation in each lineage. In addition, Sarod music is still the subject of considerable experimentation and innovation amongst younger musicians. In the immediate future, therefore, it is likely that the Sarod will witness a flowering of stylistic variety. When, or if, the Sarod too will succumb to the homogenising forces operating upon the musical culture, is impossible to predict.

The Hawaiian Slide-Guitar
The Aloha Boys of Hindustani Music

In the mid-1960s, the Hawaiian Guitar exploded upon the Hindustani music scene through the pioneering musicianship of Brij Bhushan Kabra (born: 1937). In 1968, Kabra recorded the album "Call of the Valley" with Shivkumar Sharma (Santoor) and Hariprasad Chaurasia (Flute), which won a Platinum Disc. In 1994,

another guitarist, Vishwa Mohan Bhatt (born: 1952) won a Grammy award for his collaborative ventures with Ryland Cooder, the American guitarist. And, since the dawn of the third millennium, Kabra's disciple, Debashish Bhattacharya (born: 1963) is trotting the globe, stunning the music world with Indian wizardry. The speed with which the Hawaiian slide-Guitar has transformed itself into the Indian classical guitar is phenomenal.

The Sitar climbed from relative insignificance to the peak of popularity and stature in 300 years. The Sarod did it in 150 years. The Indian slide-Guitar did it in just 30 years. But, their stories are similar: a rich indigenous tradition on similar instruments triggered off by foreign inspiration, exceptional pioneering musicianship, innovative re-engineering, and enthusiastic audience acceptance.

The Indian art music Guitar is an adaptation of the Hawaiian slide-Guitar. In the basic model, the shell of instrument is an F-hole Guitar of European design, acoustically and structurally enhanced to support a multitude of strings. But, there are several variants in circulation, with some of them sporting names suggesting the identities of their "creators".

Being a new entrant to Hindustani music, the Hawaiian slide-Guitar is still the subject of considerable experimentation and divergence in terms of acoustic design, technique and, indeed, musical idiom and style.

How it all Began

The slide-Guitar came to India before Second World War through the recordings of American guitarists, Sol Hoopii, and Joe Kaipo with Jimmie Rodgers and others. Touring Hawaiian troupes inspired local imitators. Calcutta's Aloha Boys Band, formed in 1938, was often heard on the radio. Within a generation, the Hawaiian Guitar had become a frequent feature of Indian film scores. The sound of the instrument penetrated India's musical consciousness with the prelude to the iconic semi-classical song *"Baat Chalat*

Nai Chunari Rang Dari" sung by Geeta Dutt for the film "Ladki" in 1953.

Brijbhushan Kabra

By the 1960s, the Hawaiian Guitar had found a secure home in the musical culture of Bengal, gaining popularity for instrumental renderings of Rabindra Sangeet (songs composed by Rabindranath Tagore) and of folk genres. The melodic intricacy of these genres produced a considerable resource of mature musicianship on the instrument, paved the way for its acceptance by the government-controlled broadcast media, and finally, for its entry into art music.

Although the immediate inspiration for an Indianised slide-Guitar came from North America, the instrument is the heir to an ancient Indian technique of melodic execution. There is, in fact, serious speculation that the ancient Indian slide technique played a role in the early development of the Hawaiian instrument. One Gabriel Davion, born in India, and kidnapped by a sailor to Honolulu in the late nineteenth century, is cited as the first guitarist to use the slide technique. It is conceivable that this Davion took the Indian technique to Hawaii.

The Ghoshaka Veena and the Ekatantri Veena mentioned in Indian musicological texts going back into the pre-Christian era, were both plucked instruments, on which melody was executed exactly as it is on the Hawaiian Guitar — by sliding a hard and smooth mechanical device along the strings, and not by pressing the strings between frets, as on the Spanish Guitar or the Sitar. In more recent times, the slide principle of melodic execution was represented by the Vichitra Veena in the Hindustani tradition, and by the

Gottu Vadyam (also called Chitra Veena) in the Carnatic tradition, both instruments of considerable antiquity. Despite their rarity on the contemporary concert platform, both these instruments have resisted total extinction.

The Vichitra Veena Legacy

In the Hindustani tradition, the decline of the Vichitra Veena is only partially explained by the marginalisation of the medieval Dhrupad-Dhamar genre, with which the instrument was associated. The major reasons for its decline are its unwieldy design, cumbersome technique, and an acoustic quality not particularly hospitable to electronic amplification.

The Hawaiian slide-Guitar appeared to solve all these problems simultaneously while retaining the unique capability of the Vichitra Veena — faithfully reproducing every nuance of Indian vocalism with minimum interference from the sound-priming (plucking) activity. Because of this advantage, the slide-Guitar offered a wider range of stylistic options than the Sitar and Sarod, both of which required a higher frequency of plucking.

The only trigger the Hawaiian Guitar required for claiming the Vichitra Veena's legacy was exceptional musicianship, which could demonstrate its musical potential, especially relative to the Sitar and Sarod, the frontline string instruments of the post-Independence era. The instrument found its pioneering champion in Brij Bhushan Kabra.

Vishwa Mohan Bhatt

Kabra's Contribution

Brij Bhushan, a qualified geologist, is a scion of a business family with a deep involvement in music. His father studied the Sitar under the legendary Enayet Khan, the father of Vilayat Khan. Brij Bhushan's elder brother, Damodar Lal, was a distinguished Sarod player trained by Ali Akbar Khan. In defiance of acute cynicism within the family, Brij Bhushan said an emphatic NO to the Sitar as well as the Sarod, and took on the challenge of elevating the slide-Guitar to a level of parity with them. Under the tutelage of Ali Akbar Khan, Kabra re-engineered his maverick instrument and mastered the Sarod repertoire on it. Despite guidance from a colossus amongst musicians, Kabra had to rely on his own resourcefulness for technique.

Kabra's musical vision is deeply entrenched in vocalism. He places the highest premium on the capabilities of the slide-Guitar for delivering the melodic continuity and ornamental subtleties of Hindustani vocalism. This meant the development of an idiom and technique that would minimise the frequency of strokes, and maximise the melodic execution under the impact of each stroke. These have been the guiding principles of Kabra's musical endeavours.

Kabra established himself and the Hawaiian Guitar in Hindustani music at a time when three giants of instrumental music — Vilayat Khan, Ravi Shankar, and Ali Akbar Khan — were at the peak of their creative fecundity and technical prowess. In such an environment, the mere novelty of the slide-Guitar could not have assured the instrument a future in Hindustani music. Kabra succeeded because he could exploit the uniqueness of the Hawaiian slide-Guitar as an instrument for Hindustani music.

After Kabra

In response to the changing tastes and profiles of audiences, Kabra's successors on the slide-Guitar scene have drifted away from the technical

and stylistic choices he made. The emphasis is now on heightened rhythmicality and dazzling virtuosity, rather than elaborate raga presentation and melodic richness. But, this can hardly be considered the final word on the musical destiny of so young an instrument. Whether as an acoustic machine, or as the presenter of a well-defined idiom in instrumental music, the Indian art music Guitar is still in a state of evolution. With the enthusiastic following the instrument now has in North America and Europe, its future could well be shaped by the global music market more than the Indian mainstream.

14

The Santoor
The Musical Signature of Kashmir

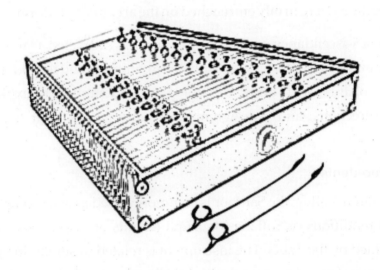

histling woods, snow-capped mountains, and rippling rivulets. If there is one instrument which projects these images of the Kashmir Valley onto your mind's eye, it is the Santoor. Until the mid-1950s, very few people outside Kashmir had heard this instrument. Today, it is difficult to find an Indian adult who has not heard it. Its status today as a concert instrument is the creation of one visionary — Shivkumar Sharma.

The Santoor is a unique instrument in Hindustani music. It is the only string instrument whose sound is activated by (percussive) impact akin to hammering. All others are either plucked or bowed.

Sharma's Santoor registered its presence on the art music scene in 1955. Its total acceptance in art music took years of struggle. But, Shivkumar and his instrument became an instant rage with composers in the film industry. The Santoor soon penetrated the public mind as the musical signature of the Kashmir Valley where many of India's feature films were shot in the 1960s. That phase of the Santoor's glory receded in the 1980s when Kashmir became unsafe, and film music started going electronic. By this time, Sharma and the Santoor were firmly entrenched on the art music platform.

Sharma's ascendancy on the art music horizon attracted a large number of musicians to the Santoor. As a result, the instrument and its idiom are now in a state of flux, with every Santoor player attempting to explore new musical directions, and redesigning the instrument to suit his musical vision.

Sufi Antecedents

In the Kashmir Valley, the Santoor is commonly used as an accompaniment for vocal renditions of Sufiana Mausiqui (chants of the sufi sects), and is accompanied by the Tabla. The instrument is related to similar instruments in the neighbouring regions of the Middle East and Central Asia. According to Sharma, similar instruments exist in Persia, Iraq, China, Tibet, Hungary, Kazakhstan, Uzbekistan, Greece, Ireland, Italy, and even in the foothills of the Alps. There exists one platform-mounted variant in central Europe, which is played in a standing position, and has foot-pedals for acoustic manipulation. This variant could be the ancestor of the Piano.

The name — Santoor — is, in all likelihood, of Sanskrit, or Persian origin. The original Sanskrit name for the instrument is "Shatatantri" (Shata = 100 +

Tantri = stringed instrument), and the Persian name, now popular, is "Santoor" (Sad or San = 100 + Toor = strings).

After studying this family of instruments in several parts of the world, Sharma discovered that the Indian (Kashmiri) Santoor is the only one with exactly hundred strings (Interview with the author on 2 December 2003). According to him, Persian experts are unable to explain why their Santoor with only 72 strings has a name suggesting 100 strings. Sharma also finds it interesting that ancient Indian texts have referred to the Shatatantri as being used for accompaniment to the chanting of mantras (religious chants), this being also the purpose for which the instrument is used in the Kashmir Valley.

Shivkumar's Odyssey

Shivkumar was ideally suited for his pioneering role because he had received early training in vocal music, and had established himself as a Tabla player of eminence before defecting to the Santoor. His mastery over melody and rhythm enabled him to develop a balanced melodic-rhythmic idiom, which astutely exploits the essential rhythmicality of the Santoor, while also neutralising it.

Sharma took up the Santoor upon the insistence of his father, Umadatta Sharma, a Tabla exponent and a vocalist. During his tenure as Chief Producer of music on Kashmir Radio, Umadatta heard the Santoor, and saw in it a challenge worthy of his son. The relatively unrefined instrument Shivkumar

Shivkumar Sharma

inherited from the sufi tradition was incapable of delivering contemporary raga-based music in an electronically engineered environment. However, that was the very instrument on which Shivkumar practised, and made his debut as a Santoor exponent.

The world of art music was unimpressed because of its obvious limitations in the handling of melodic nuances. This triggered off Sharma's efforts at re-engineering the instrument and developing an idiom aimed at exploiting its unique character, while also enhancing its melodic capabilities.

Sharma re-engineered the instrument in all important aspects, modified the placement, posture and tuning, and also developed a new stroke-craft system for the music he wanted to play on it. With these innovations, the instrument acquired a satisfactory output for the contemporary acoustic environment, while also defining a distinctive musical experience.

Shivkumar's contribution has woven the music of the instrument intimately into the fabric of modern Hindustani music, while also shaping an independent genre for it. This genre has clear reference points in the music of the plucked lutes. His achievements have made the Santoor the best known Indian instrument outside India, next only to the Sitar, the Sarod, and the Tabla.

The Santoor after Shivkumar Sharma

Sharma's rise to the peak of the profession attracted a sizeable inflow of fresh talent to the instrument. The booming demand for Santoor training led aspirants to many teachers who probably qualified as musicians, but not as Santoor players. Other than his son, Rahul, Shivkumar himself has accepted very few disciples. While the popular segment of the music industry features quite a few competent Santoor exponents, an exponent of Shivkumar's calibre is not yet visible on the art music horizon.

Sharma's music is exemplary for its adherence to raga grammar and the orthodox architecture of the music of the major plucked instruments (Sitar and Sarod). Sharma's approach to music represents a fine balance between the melodic and rhythmic elements. He has exploited the rhythmic potential of the instrument astutely, without allowing it to interfere with his refinement of its melodic capabilities and expressions.

The succeeding generation of Santoor players has, interestingly, developed a libertarian and pupulist approach to the content of their music.

In terms of style, Sharma's successors are exploring two principal directions — the percussive-rhythmic direction derived from the Tabla and directions inspired by the keyboard-based Piano. The Tabla direction underutilises the melodic potential of the Santoor while the Piano direction demands far more from the Santoor than it can possibly deliver.

The recent histories of the Sitar and Sarod would suggest that any instrument achieves stylistic maturity only after several generations of musicians, representing different backgrounds, have contributed to its development. Shivkumar Sharma picked up an obscure regional instrument, and gave it stature comparable to the more mature instruments. Even if the immediate post-Sharma directions appear mystifying, the Santoor is now firmly established in Hindustani music.

15

The Tanpura and Swaramandal
The Pillars and Laptops
of Hindustani Vocalism

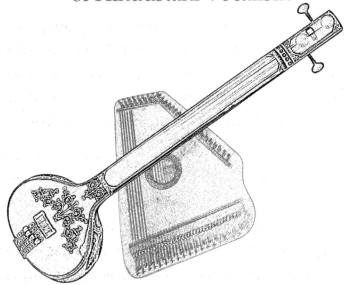

They are ubiquitous. Tall pillars mounted on large bulbous bases. You have seen two of them behind every Hindustani vocalist — sometimes four. They are Tanpuras. Some call them Tambouras. Far less frequently than the pillars, you may have seen the laptop that vocalists use during a concert. It is called a Swaramandal. The instrument either lies horizontally in the vocalist's lap, or stands upright across his chest. Neither of these instruments produces any melody or rhythm. And, it is fair to ask why they are there.

The Tanpura/Tamboura

The word Tanpura derives from two components: Tan = melodic phrase + Purak = that which completes or complements. The name describes the

Salamat Ali and Nazakat Ali Khan

function of filling the silences, and providing continuity to the musical experience. Neither the word Tanpura, nor its scientific nomenclature (drone) can, however, do justice to the hallowed position it enjoys, and the importance of its role.

The Tanpura evolved from the idea of supporting a vocal rendition with the "adhara swara" — the foundation note or scale base to which the musician is singing. The sustained presence of the foundation note helps him to achieve a higher degree of pitch-precision in his recital. But, more importantly, melodic music — such as Hindustani music, in fact, Indian music in general — acquires its meaning only with reference to the foundation note. The support of the foundation note is therefore crucial to delivering the musical meaning of the performance to its listeners.

But, if this was all a vocalist wanted, it was not necessary to have so complicated an instrument as the Tanpura. The folk and tribal traditions have for long used simple instruments which have done this job pretty well in their environments. Some of these instruments are fairly refined in their acoustic design, though falling far short of the contemporary Tanpura. The beauty of the Tanpura's output is that it remains unobtrusive while aiding the music-making process. At its best, the sound of a perfectly tuned Tanpura is a near-mystical experience — it transports the musician into a trance-like state, and focuses his energies on the process of creation.

The present-day Tanpura represents a maturation of two streams of evolution. One is a folk stream of instruments which have existed in India from times immemorial. Many of them, like the Ektara (single-stringed instrument), can still be heard all over India, with bards and minstrels singing to its accompaniment. The second stream of evolution is traced to the Tamboura, an instrument that came from Persia in the eleventh century CE.

The Tamboura from Persia was a fretted instrument on which melody was played. It became an important part of its musical activities at the Delhi court from the thirteenth century. However, by the early seventeenth century, two types of Tambour, similar in structure, were being used — a fretted one on which melody could be played, and a fretless one which played no melody. The fretted one may have been a forerunner of the Sitar, and the fretless version could have been a nascent Tanpura.

The Tanpura development obviously answered an emerging musical need. Once the need was recognised, the instrument was progressively refined to achieve higher levels of sophistication. Physicists, starting from Sir C.V. Raman, have long been intrigued by the Tanpura's acoustic qualities, and have invested a great deal of experimental effort into it.

The present-day Tanpura has four strings (sometimes five or even six), which are plucked sequentially. Despite this, the output of the strings is not sequential. It flows out in overlapping harmonic waves, which are in acoustic consonance with one another. In effect, what the Tanpura generates is a rhythm-neutral and cyclical harmonic ambience, compatible with the chosen foundation note, without delivering the foundation note itself. This acoustic phenomenon is created by the design of the Tanpura frame, the special technique of fine-tuning the platform on which the strings are set, the fingering technique, and the acoustic properties of the "tumba", sourced ideally from Pandharpur in Maharashtra. The Tanpura is, in fact,

acknowledged by the music world as a uniquely Indian masterpiece of acoustic design.

The eminent musicologist, Ashok Ranade, suggests that the need for such an instrument may have surfaced with the ascendancy of Khayal vocalism, with its dominant role for the improvisatory process, and vast scope for individual creativity. Little wonder then, that the greatest vocalists of the twentieth century worked closely with Tanpura-makers of Miraj (southern Maharashtra) to help upgrade the acoustic quality of the instruments made in that city.

Bade Gulam Ali Khan

With the growing travel needs of musicians, the search began for portable and convenient alternatives. Smaller Tanpuras, called Tanpuris, were in existence, and had a small following — mainly among instrumentalists. A more portable alternative was attempted with the Box Tanpura, designed by Bishandas Sharma of Delhi. The Box Tanpura has four strings mounted atop a rectangular wooden box less than half the height of a conventional Tanpura. Another convenience to emerge in this segment was a south Indian innovation — the Sruti Box, a bellows-driven drone about half the size of an executive briefcase. It is sound-primed intermittently like a Harmonium. In recent years, the Sruti Box has gone electronic, and electronic Tanpuras have also arrived, thus providing hands-free options. Each of these substitutes is being re-engineered constantly in the hope of dislodging the conventional Tanpura from the concert platform, but with only limited success so far.

The Swaramandal

The influential users of the Swaramandal in recent years have been Bade Ghulam Ali Khan and Kishori Amonkar. Though their example has inspired several other vocalists, the instrument is still a rarity in India. Pakistani vocalists, however, appear to use it more widely than Indian vocalists do.

The Swaramandal is a harp, most probably of Indian origin. Some authorities equate it with the Mattakokila, a string instrument mentioned in pre-Christian literature. By the thirteenth century, the Swaramandal had become an important accompaniment instrument in Indian music. It is a trapezoid wooden box, with twenty-one to thirty-six metal strings strung across its top. The strings are tuned to the scale of the raga being performed, and plucked with the help of a wire plectrum worn on the fingers.

Although it is capable of playing formal music as much as any harp is, it has been used primarily for occasional strumming to fill the silences in a vocal music rendition. While every vocalist has his or her style of playing this instrument, hardly anyone tries to do more with it than filling silences. This is understandable because most vocalists have a Sarangi or a Harmonium providing melodic accompaniment.

Since the Tanpura and the Swaramandal are used together and are both silence fillers — amongst other functions — a comparison between them deserves attention.

The Tanpura is played continuously during a rendition, while the Swaramandal is played only intermittently and briefly at each activation. The Tanpura is normally tuned to two fixed points — the scale base and the mid-octave point, while the Swaramandal is tuned to the scale of the chosen raga across almost three octaves. The Tanpura does not deliver notes in perceptible sequence, while the Swaramandal does. Because of its acoustic design, however, the musical experience of the Swaramandal is more a suggestion of

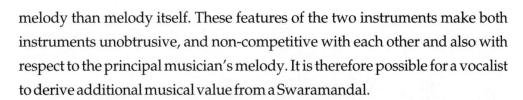

melody than melody itself. These features of the two instruments make both instruments unobtrusive, and non-competitive with each other and also with respect to the principal musician's melody. It is therefore possible for a vocalist to derive additional musical value from a Swaramandal.

What if a vocalist wants to use a Swaramandal but cannot find a competent Tanpura accompanist? Once again, Bishandas Sharma provided a solution. He enlarged the width of his Box Tanpura to mount a limited Swaramandal type assembly on one side and a full-fledged Tanpura assembly on the other. On this hybrid, called a Swarasangam, a vocalist can play the Tanpura with one hand, and the Swaramandal with the other.

The Vocalist's Mai-Baap

The great Dhrupad vocalist, Nasir Aminuddin Dagar, once described his pair of Tanpuras as his "Mai-Baap" (mother and father). This observation could justify the space devoted to this seemingly unimportant musical instrument, and the time you have invested reading this introduction. The Tanpura is, in fact, so fundamental to Hindustani vocal music, that you cannot imagine its present-day sophistication without its support. The Swaramandal, on the other hand, is an optional enrichment of the musical experience, without which a vast majority of Indian vocalists — and their audiences — seem quite happy.

16

The Sarangi
Awaiting a State Funeral

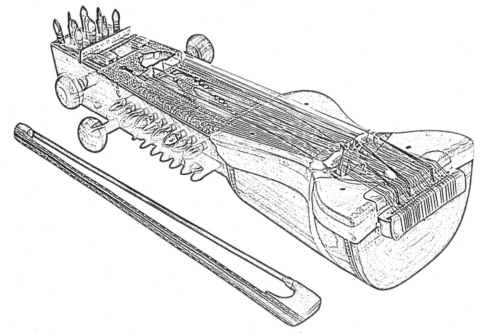

The Sarangi is an unsung hero of the Golden Age of vocal music (mid-nineteenth to mid-twentieth century) in the Hindustani tradition. Valued for delivering the closest possible approximation to the human voice, the Sarangi has been the most favoured accompaniment to vocal music. In recent years, the instrument has also attempted to create a solo status for itself. In both these roles, it now faces an uncertain future.

The Sarangi is related to the Pinaki Veena and the Ravanahasta, two instruments encountered in Hindu mythology. It is found in various forms all over the Indian subcontinent. Unlike several other major instruments in Hindustani music (e.g. Sitar, Sarod), the Sarangi family is entirely of Indian origin, with virtually no trace of foreign influence.

Its emergence is traced to folk traditions, in which wandering bards and minstrels hung the instrument around their neck, and accompanied themselves on it. The instrument became an accompanist to art music probably in the seventeenth century. Today, the family includes a wide range of designs, from the single-string tribal instrument to the sophisticated art music Sarangi, which evolved around CE 1850, with Meerut (UP) as the principal centre of manufacturing.

In the Mainstream

The Sarangi entered the mainstream through enterprising bards drifting towards the feudal courts to make a living as accompanists to courtesans. In due course, they became custodians of the vocalist arts, and teachers of courtesans, with a share in the revenues of the salons. In this role, the Sarangi steadily enlarged its presence to become the preferred accompaniment for female as well as male singers. The only vocal genre to have steadfastly avoided the Sarangi, and also any other melodic accompaniment, is Dhrupad.

A life in the courtesan districts gave Sarangi players, and the instrument, a stigma that it could not shed until it was too late. In the late nineteenth/early twentieth century, social reformist movements backed by the Victorian morals of India's colonial rulers, pushed the institution of courtesans to the brink. Although art music was not their target, the movement severely dented the Sarangi, which depended largely on the world of courtesans for its sustenance. The deathblow, however, came from the Harmonium, invented in Paris (1840), which caught on speedily as a replacement for the Sarangi.

Response to the Harmonium Challenge

The Harmonium's acoustic design made it unsuitable for Hindustani music. However, it was untainted by social stigma, and had several practical advantages. Being an easier instrument to master, the Harmonium created an ample supply of accompanists, who were cheaper to hire. For performers in the lighter genres, the Harmonium was a greater boon because the vocalist could master the instrument, and dispense with the accompanist altogether.

Towards the end of the nineteenth century, the declining fortunes of the Sarangi gave rise to two significant developments. Several exceptional Sarangi players abandoned the Sarangi in favour of a career as vocalists. This phenomenon gave India some of its finest twentieth-century vocalists. The other significant development was the emergence of the Sarangi soloist. In the 1920s, Bundu Khan (died: 1955), the finest Sarangi player of the period, started recording 78 rpm discs of solo performances. In later years, several other Sarangi players also published solo recordings.

Ramnarain

In the post-Independence period, Ramnarain (born: 1927) has been the most significant Sarangi player to bid farewell to accompaniment, and turn soloist. He is largely responsible for creating an international constituency for the Sarangi, and reviving interest in the art amongst scions of the Sarangi playing families.

In the next generation, Sultan Khan, a distinguished accompanist and soloist, has attempted a revival of the original model of the bards by turning

vocalist and accompanying himself on the Sarangi — an option not available to every Sarangi player.

Sultan Khan

In the succeeding generation, the most successful soloist has been Dhruva Ghosh (born: 1957), trained by Mohammad Sagiruddin Khan, one of the finest Sarangi players of recent times. Dhruva has not shunned accompaniment, but enlarged the niche for Sarangi solos, especially in the international market, by exploring unorthodox stylistic directions.

These individual achievements do not, evidently, symbolise a revival in the fortunes of the Sarangi. The accompaniment market has been lost to the Harmonium. The All India Radio, which supported the Sarangi by banning the Harmonium, has now lifted the ban. The popular music industry, once a significant user of Sarangi talent, has shifted almost totally to electronic music. The population of competent Sarangi players is shrinking along with the demand for their art.

The Sarangi: As the Accompanist and Soloist

Essentially, the melodic accompaniment (Sarangi or Harmonium) is intended to fill the silences that a vocal rendition creates. Beyond this, the accompaniment function is amenable to a bewildering variety of descriptions. In its ideal manifestation, the Sarangi-accompanied vocal concert is a partnership of equals.

As a solo artist, the Sarangi player has no vocalist to follow, support, or guide. Despite this, he is obliged to work within the framework of vocal genres because his instrument is designed explicitly as a worthy vehicle for the modern genres of vocal music. These realities impose handicaps, and also offer some advantages.

The handicap lies in having to render a genre of vocal music without the spoken word. Performing a vocal genre of music without these articulations poses a challenge to the attention-holding power of a Sarangi solo. As a soloist, the Sarangi player compensates for the handicap by focusing on his freedom to exploit the technical capabilities of his instrument.

Contemporary Sarangi solos appear to follow a combination of two approaches for this purpose. One approach is to stretch the melodic complexity to a level which a vocalist is either unable to match, or will not attempt out of fear of sounding un-musical. Such intimidating virtuosity is conspicuous in the music of Ramnarain. The other approach is to incorporate musical ideas borrowed from the plucked instruments (Sitar/Sarod). This latter approach is prominent in the solo renditions of Dhruva Ghosh.

With its continued anchoring in the modern genres of vocal music, the Sarangi cannot be said, yet, to have evolved a distinctive language for solo performance. However, even at the present stage of its evolution, a solo by a mature Sarangi player can be a memorable experience.

The Prospects for the Sarangi Soloist

At the present juncture, available quality solos are predominantly of Sarangi players who have also distinguished themselves as accompanists. Their calibre as soloists rests on a musical vision that has been enriched, rather than blurred, by providing accompaniment to a diversity of vocalists performing different styles and genres.

The loss of the accompaniment market to the Harmonium hits the Sarangi's future in two ways: It evaporates an important part of the livelihood for Sarangi players. So, the supply of Sarangi players is shrinking.

If the total resource of musicianship is shrinking, the emergence of soloists from that pool is likely to be poorer in terms of numbers as well as quality. Secondly, it deprives Sarangi players of a significant component of the maturation process involved in accompaniment. This is yet another reason why the musicianship of soloists emerging in the future could be inferior.

Dhruva Ghosh

The evolution of a domestic market for Sarangi solos has not been helped by the government-owned broadcast media. Every time the state declares a period of national mourning for a departed dignitary, the only music you hear on All India Radio and Doordarshan for a whole week, is a wailing alap performed on the Sarangi. By a single stroke of a bureaucrat's pen, an instrument that was the soul of the entertainment districts in feudal India has been decreed an instrument for mourning. Considering that these government institutions once protected the Sarangi against the onslaught of the Harmonium, nothing could be more ironical than the Sarangi itself being given a state funeral.

Growing international interest in the Sarangi has inspired a few young Sarangi players to shun accompaniment altogether, and aim directly for a career as soloists. Whether such a route can deliver a sufficient pool of competent soloists is debatable. The domestic market for Sarangi solos is still unproven. The international market, still nascent, can be very selective, and also amazingly fickle. These factors only compound the risk of emerging career strategies.

The Sarangi's future is thus doubly clouded — as the second fiddle, and the first.

17

The Violin
A Gift of the Carnatic Tradition to Hindustani Music

There is one musician whom Lord Yehudi Menuhin, the iconic Western violinist, never failed to meet and hear during his trips to India — the violinist, M.S. Gopalakrishnan. Interestingly, Gopalakrishnan commands equal stature amongst Carnatic and Hindustani connoisseurs. His musical persona virtually sums up the story of the Violin in Indian art music.

How it All Began

The Violin came to India with European colonists — the French in Pondicherry, the Portuguese in Goa, and the British in Bengal. It was introduced to Indian art music by Baluswamy Dikshitar (1786-1858), a brother of the legendary Carnatic composer, Muthuswamy Dikshitar. Baluswamy heard the Violin in a British band, noted its acoustic closeness to the human voice and thought it well suited for accompanying Carnatic vocalism. His father sent Baluswamy as well as Muthuswamy to study the Violin under the band master at Fort William. In 1884, Vadivelu, a disciple of the Dikshitar family, introduced the Violin to an enthusiastic response at the Travancore court. Around the same time, the Maratha princes of Tanjore also discovered the promise of the instrument, and encouraged its adoption. Since then, several generations of violinists have worked to make the Violin a major instrument in Carnatic music.

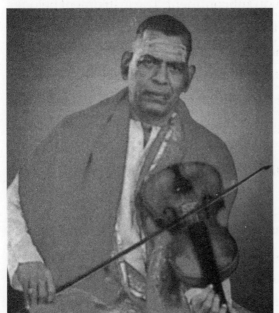

M.S. Gopalakrishanan

The instrument entered Hindustani music in the 1930s through the initiatives of Allauddin Khan (Baba), Vishnu Digambar Paluskar, S.N. Ratanjankar, and Gajananrao Joshi.

Amongst the several instruments he had mastered, Allauddin Khan had also studied the Violin under Mr. Lobo, the conductor of the Eden Gardens Band in Calcutta. Baba published the first ever Violin recording of Hindustani music on a 78 rpm disc, thus heralding its arrival in the

Hindustani mainstream. In later years, his disciple, Timir Baran, introduced the Violin to film industry orchestration, and another disciple, V.G. Jog, emerged as a towering violinist.

Around the same time, Vishnu Digambar invited Parur Sundaram Iyer, an eminent Carnatic violinist (the father of M.S. Gopalakrishnan) to teach at Gandharva Mahavidyalaya, India's first music university. A few years later, S.N. Ratanjankar, the principal of the Maris College of Music at Lucknow (now Bhatkhande University), invited V.G. Jog to teach at the institution. The feudal chieftain of Aundh in Maharashtra virtually ordered Gajananrao Joshi, an eminent vocalist of the Gwalior Gharana, to master the Violin — which he did without a teacher, and later groomed several young violinists.

Not Really a Foreign Instrument

The Violin has its origins in the Indian subcontinent. The instrument belongs to an ancient family of bowed lutes traced to the Ravanhasta, featured in Indian mythology. This family includes a large number of folk and tribal instruments, as also the sophisticated Sarangi. Remarkably Violin-like instruments are depicted amongst the sculptures of the Mallikarjuna temple (Vijayawada, tenth century), and the Nataraja temple (Chidambaram, twelfth century). The ancestor of the contemporary Violin travelled from India to Europe through the Middle East and Central Asia.

Until the acceptance of the bowed instruments in art music, the Hindustani and Carnatic traditions both gave pride of place to the Veena as an accompanist to vocal music. Once Violin accompaniment partially replaced the Veena, it was also able to emerge as a solo instrument in Carnatic music. When the Violin entered Hindustani music — almost three generations after its Carnatic debut — the Sarangi was the preferred accompaniment, but fast losing ground to the Harmonium. Hindustani music thus ended up reserving the Violin for solo performance, and only sporadically as an accompaniment.

For evolving into a mature instrument for Indian art music, the violin has thus had much more time and much wider exposure in the Carnatic tradition, than in Hindustani music. Little wonder then that Hindustani music remains indebted to Carnatic music for the art of the Violin.

The Violin in Hindustani Music

Gajananrao Joshi (1911-87), the pioneer of the Violin in Maharashtra, performed predominantly as a vocalist. However, he groomed several younger violinists, amongst whom Shridhar Parsekar (1920-64) built a formidable reputation. Parsekar died young, and Joshi's other disciples either became teachers or made a living in the popular music industry. As a result, the Gajananrao lineage of violinists is no longer represented on the art music platform.

Amongst Hindustani violinists, V.G. Jog (1922-2004) enjoyed the longest innings at the top of the league. Jog had his early training with S.C. Athavale, Ganpatrao Purohit, Vishweshwar Shastry, and S.N. Ratanjankar. He later trained with Allauddin Khan, and took a degree in music from the Maris

College of Music. From 1953 till retirement, Jog served on the staff of All India Radio.

Jog performed in the vocal Khayal and Thumree, as well as the Tantakari idiom — the idiom of the plucked instruments, the Sitar and Sarod. His Khayal style was a mix of Gwalior, Agra and the eclectic Bhaskarbuwa Bakhle styles of vocalism.

In the next generation, the most venerated violinist is M.S.

V.G. Jog

Gopalakrishnan (born: 1931), popularly called MSG. He studied the Violin in the Carnatic and Hindustani traditions with his father, Parur Sundaram Iyer. After his father's demise, he studied Kairana Gharana (Hindustani) vocalism with Guru Krishnananda. He also took an eight-month course in the Western Violin technique at the Musee Musicale at Madras.

He exploded onto the Hindustani music scene in his early youth, accompanying leading vocalist like Omkarnath Thakur, D.V. Paluskar and Bade Ghulam Ali Khan. His trajectory in Carnatic music was equally sensational. Despite a less frequent presence on the Hindustani platform, his name spells magic amongst connoisseurs in both the traditions.

D.K. Datar

MSG presents Hindustani music in the Khayal style as well as the Tantakari idioms. He is respected for the neatness of architecture, and authentic treatment of musical material in both the traditions. In addition, MSG is revered for his flawless bowing technique, on par with the best in the world.

In the same generation as MSG, the Paluskar tradition of the Violin is represented by D.K. Datar (born: 1932). He studied the Violin under Vighneshwara Shastry, and vocal music under his uncle, D.V. Paluskar. Expectedly, Datar has remained faithful to the vocalised idiom of the Gwalior Gharana during his long career as a violinist.

The Carnatic tradition continues to lead the Hindustani art through N. Rajam (born: 1938). She studied Carnatic music under her violinist father, Narayana Iyer, and the famous vocalist, Musiri Subramaniam Iyer. While still in her teens, she became a concert performer and accompanist to the tallest Carnatic vocalists, including M.S. Subbulakshmi.

When her family moved to Bombay, she enrolled as a private (off campus) student for a degree from the Banaras Hindu University (BHU), where Omkarnth Thakur headed the Faculty of Music. She began intermittent training with him during his visits to Bombay. Soon, she began accompanying him regularly. Later she joined BHU as a lecturer, and flowered as a performer, teacher, and academician under her mentor's supervision. She no longer performs Carnatic music.

Omkarnath publicly acknowledged that Rajam understood his music best and followed it most faithfully. This is significant, because his was an emotionally charged style, rich in the manipulation of timbre and volume. In Omkarnath's music, the highly evolved technique of Carnatic violinists found a fresh challenge, which Rajam conquered. In this, and several other respects, Rajam is credited with bringing the Hindustani Violin idiom and technique closer to the experience of vocalism than ever before.

This overview suggests that the Violin started in Hindustani music as an exponent of the vocal idiom (Gajananrao Joshi and Parsekar), was tempted — like the Flute and the Sarangi — to venture into the Tantakar idiom (Jog and MSG), and has now returned to the vocalised idiom (D.K. Datar and N. Rajam). Despite the immense influence of Rajam, hers may not be the final verdict on the idiomatic destiny of the instrument in the Hindustani tradition. As we have seen (see chapters on the Bansuri and the Sarangi), rival idioms do hold some appeal for performers on the bow and wood-wind instruments.

The Hindustani Violin Today

Rajam is acknowledged as the foremost Hindustani violinist today. In the next generation, the significant Hindustani violinists are both Rajam's disciples — her daughter, Sangeeta Shankar, and her niece, Kala Ramnath, who later became a disciple of the distinguished vocalist, Jasraj. In a sense, quality Hindustani musicianship on the Violin is presently the domain of Carnatic expertise.

N. Rajam

Is it then to be expected that future generations of outstanding Hindustani violinists will also emerge from the Carnatic tradition? Not necessarily, says Sangeeta Shankar, who is also an authority on the history of the Violin in Indian art music (interview with the author on 15 July 2011). She admits that Carnatic violinists have a head start because of their superior technique, evolved over a longer history of involvement. But exceptional musicianship, she argues, will always create a place for itself. And, fine musicians could emerge from anywhere. As possible nurseries, she points towards Maharashtra and Bengal, both of which have a visible base of students pursuing the art, and even towards a small group of Western violinists seriously pursuing Hindustani music.

Sangeeta's observations — valid as they are — need to be considered against the absence of a "Violin culture" which can nurture quality musicians for Hindustani music.

To begin with, the bowed instruments — as a category — now occupy only a small corner on the Hindustani music platform. Even at the top, the

Sangeeta Shankar

"market" for the Violin does not have enough room to support full-time performing careers. The government-owned broadcast media, once significant employers of violinists, are shrinking avenues. The popular music industry, a major source of livelihood for violinists till recently, has gone electronic. Very few schools, colleges or universities outside south India employ violin teachers.

The Hindustani tradition has not adopted the Violin as standard accompaniment to vocal music. Thus, an important avenue of livelihood and an irreplaceable aid to artistic maturation has been denied to Hindustani violinists. Adding to these factors is the cost of owning a concert quality instrument, which far exceeds the costs of the more popular instruments like the Sitar and the Sarod. These realities define an eco-system not particularly conducive to a steady supply of quality violinists.

Considering its musical value and its achievements so far, it is not reasonable to dismiss the violin as a mere footnote in the history of Hindustani music. It is, of course, also difficult to identify forces that can propel it forward. Violin enthusiasts hope that Hindustani music will continue to attract quality violinists from the Carnatic culture at least for a few more generations.

18

The Bansuri
A Humble Bamboo Flute
in a Highbrow Avatar

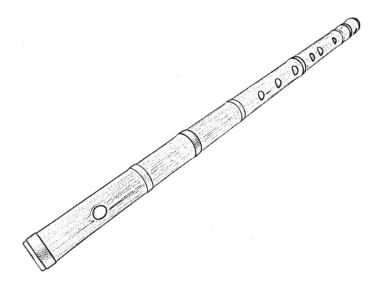

The Bansuri (the bamboo Flute) enjoys such formidable status on the current musical scene, that one would imagine this has always been so. In reality, despite Lord Krishna's blessings bestowed upon it several millennia ago, the instrument was elevated to the concert platform only in the mid-twentieth century. The development was pioneered by Pannalal Ghosh (1911-60), and consolidated by subsequent generations of flautists.

The Bansuri is easily the most widely played instrument in India. Starting in the pre-Christian era, it has been present in all segments of the musical culture. Even in the art music segment, where it had a negligible presence till recently, it has enjoyed a large base of amateur musicianship. The reasons for its popularity are obvious. It is an instrument of simple construction with no moving parts, made from easily available materials, and has fixed holes for the notes, thus making melody reasonably easy to handle. In addition, it is portable, immune to climatic variations, and does not require maintenance or periodic overhaul by expert craftsmen. And, finally — this too matters — even a professional quality Flute is a relatively inexpensive proposition. This brings access, and a basic level of competence within widespread reach. Elevating it to the concert platform in its historical context, however, took a lot more than this.

The Context

The bamboo Flute is so pervasive, comes in so many different sizes and designs, and is known by so many names, that its authoritative history is impossible to construct. Fragments of information are, however, available for tracing its trajectory.

In the Vedic era, the bamboo Flute was an important accompaniment to religious rites and rituals. Up to the thirteenth century, musicological literature has given detailed descriptions of the instrument, its design, construction and playing technique. Till this period, it would appear, the instrument enjoyed considerable popularity for solo performance and accompaniment. Its fortunes declined probably during the Mughal period.

Amongst the instruments, Akbar's chief musician, Miya Tansen, was partial to the string instruments — the Rudra Veena and the Rabab. During Jehangir's reign, there is one solitary report of a flautist having been honoured at the court. Highbrow music admitted a wood-wind instrument in the seventeenth century, when the Shehnai became an integral part of court ceremonies. During the eighteenth and nineteenth centuries, Tansen's descendants remained influential, and propagated the string instruments. The trend continued under the titled aristocracy in British India. Feudal patronage was important in that era because the courts were the only institutions where a large number of musicians interacted, and validated each other's art. Thus, for more than 500 years, the Bansuri remained isolated from the mainstream of highbrow music.

During Akbar's reign, but independently of the Mughal court, the Bansuri received a huge impetus from the Bhakti movement. Poets of the movement wove the Bansuri intimately into the romance of Radha and Krishna. This resulted in an explosion of popular interest in the Bansuri. But, it only strengthened the Bansuri's presence in middle-brow and low-brow territory. As a result, when Pannalal Ghosh launched his career as a soloist in the 1930s, he was confronted with a folk instrument — at best an amateur instrument — of shrill sound and limited melodic capability.

Pannalal Ghosh

Pannalal Ghosh started playing the Sitar and the Bansuri at a young age, with a stronger interest in the Bansuri. Forced by economic necessity, he joined the film music industry at the age of 23. Alongside his profession, he studied the Harmonium with Khushi Muhammad, vocal music with the legendary Girija Shankar Chakravarty, and launched himself as a solo flautist. He soon found it difficult to juggle his profession with his passion. At the age of 36, he quit films and became a disciple of Allauddin Khan, a master of several instruments, though a performer on the Sarod. Pannalal's

Pannalal Ghosh

grooming gave him a solid foundation in the major genres. His musical vision now required a worthy vehicle. So, he worked systematically on the design of the instrument.

He experimented with a variety of materials — steel, brass, chrome, wood, bamboo, and even polymers. He finally settled on bamboo from India's north-east for its acoustic properties. He then enhanced the length of the Flute substantially, with a corresponding enlargement of the diameter. He increased the total number of holes on the tube from seven to eight. This gave him a comfortable range of two-and-a-half octaves. For deep lower octave melody, he designed a bass Flute, larger and wider than the regular instrument. To manage these innovations, he also had to devise a new fingering technique. The pair of flutes he designed is now virtually the "industry standard".

With this equipment, he was able to spearhead the Flute renaissance in Hindustani music. He was the first significant musician to introduce the sitar-style alap-jod-jhala form to the Flute idiom. He was equally competent in the obvious idiom of the wood-wind instruments — Khayal, Thumree, and folk music. His versatility of style and content was passed on to his principal disciples.

The Bansuri after Pannalal Ghosh

In the next generation, Devendra Murdheshwar (Ghosh's disciple), and, Vijay Raghav Rao (a disciple of Ravi Shankar) were the leading flautists. They brought the Flute idiom closer to the Sitar/Sarod idiom. This trend continued in the third generation, primarily with Raghunath Seth and Hariprasad Chaurasia.

Hariprasad Chaurasia (born: 1938) studied the Flute under Bholanath Prasanna at Allahabad, and qualified as an empanelled artist on All India Radio (AIR). Thereafter, he joined the staff of AIR, Cuttack, where his duties included accompanying a variety of artists in light and folk music. When he moved to AIR, Bombay, the world of film music welcomed him enthusiastically because of his technical command over the instrument, and stylistic versatility. He could soon quit his AIR job to make headway as an art music soloist, while continuing his involvement with films. His potential as an art music flautist was honed and unleashed in Bombay by his last Guru, Annapoorna Devi, daughter of Allauddin Khan. With this grooming, Chaurasia catapulted himself and the Bansuri onto the global concert platform.

Stylistic Directions

Chaurasia's last Guru, Annapoorna Devi, belongs to a lineage specialising in the string instruments, and is herself an outstanding Surbahar player. Her father had trained Pannalal Ghosh, Ali Akbar Khan, Ravi Shankar and Nikhil Bannerjee, amongst others. A significant consequence of Chaurasia's apprenticeship with her was that the influence of the Sitar/Sarod idiom over the Flute now became even stronger.

It has been argued that legitimate idiom of a breath-driven instrument is continuous melody, and not the discontinuous melody produced on the plucked

Hariprasad Chaurasia

instrumeints. But, you cannot argue with success. The drift towards the Sitar/Sarod idiom did, indeed, help the emergence of Pannalal Ghosh, and its reinforcement has paid rich dividends to his successors and the Flute. This trend warrants a brief re-look at history.

The wood-wind instruments, as a category, have for long enjoyed only a small share of the classical music market. The causes for this phenomenon are partly historical. For over half a millennium, the princely courts neglected the wood-wind instruments. The Shehnai, the more fortunate of the two, had only an inferior status as a provider of background music to ceremonies, and not that of a concert instrument which commands an attentive audience.

The string instruments — beneficiaries of prolonged feudal patronage — became even more dominant after the advent of the microphone, to the extent of surpassing vocal music in popularity. By the time of Pannalal Ghosh's arrival, instrumental music had become almost synonymous with the Sitar or the Sarod. In such an environment, it is easy to appreciate why Ghosh and his successors have been rewarded for plugging their music into the dominant "model" of instrumental music.

A similar story might be unfolding in the bowed instruments — specifically the Sarangi and the Violin. These instruments are also designed for melodic continuity, and the vocal idiom is their "natural" habitat. They too have had a small share of the market. The directions chosen by contemporary maestros of the bowed instruments suggest that these instruments are also moving — in their own distinctive manner — closer to the idiom of the Sitar and the Sarod in order to avert further marginalisation.

These observations point towards the awesome strength of the homogenising forces operating within the musical culture. Stylistic diversity now appears to risk audience rejection not only within the realm of each instrument, but even across instruments. This cannot augur well either for this individualistic art or its rich legacy of musical instruments.

19

The Shehnai
Gasping for Breath

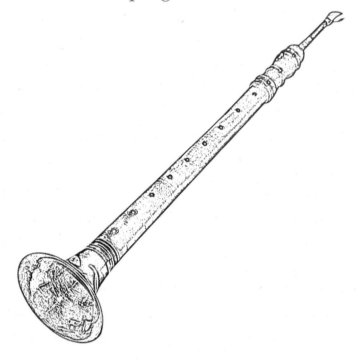

Only two generations ago, the Shehnai was perhaps the most widely heard instrument in northern India. It has, for long, been an integral part of tribal, folk, religious and ceremonial music on the subcontinent. In the latter half of the twentieth century, Bismillah Khan (1916-2006) took it to the peak of popularity on the concert platform. By the time of Bismillah Khan's departure, however, the instrument was gasping for breath.

Instruments of the Shehnai family are found in all parts of India. Nagaswaram, an instrument of the same family, and known by several names, has comparable status in India's southern peninsula. Even in north India, the instrument has several names, each suggesting a different facet of the instrument's personality. Despite confusing signals regarding its origins, scholars believe that the Shehnai is an entirely Indian instrument.

Idiom and Repertoire

Being a breath-driven instrument, the Shehnai's natural expression is continuous melody. This is why Shehnai music is driven by the vocal genres of music. In recent years, the musical culture of Bismillah Khan's home, Benares, has largely influenced the repertoire of Shehnai players on the Hindustani music platform. The Khayal format has traditionally been the primary vehicle for raga presentation. The semi-classical repertoire is dominated by the prevalent genres of the Purab (Eastern UP) region such as Bol-banao Thumree and seasonal songs such as the

Bismillah Khan

Kajri, Chaiti, Hori, Jhoola, Phagun, Sawan, etc. Shehnai players from other regions, primarily Maharashtra, have adopted Bismillah Khan's repertoire, but also tended to include local folk and regional music such as Lavani, and Natya Sangeet.

An important facet of the Shehnai music is that its practitioners make their living performing at religious ceremonies, mainly weddings. In the post-Independence era, hardly any Shehnai player has been able to make a living entirely on the art music platform. In the ceremonial context, the audience is primarily of people unlettered in classical music. In addition, the Shehnai provides only background music to the ceremony, with hardly anybody paying attention to its music. The Shehnai player's audience is thus mostly uncultivated, involuntary and inattentive. Registering his presence, therefore, obliges the Shehnai player to play music that is dominated by popular or folk flavours.

This configuration of circumstances influences the Shehnai player's approach to handling serious raga-based music when he does perform it. Even the most respected Shehnai players can sometimes be faulted on their raga grammar, and for flirting with popular and folk expressions in renderings of art music. The innate populism of Shehnai players has contributed immensely to its success on the concert platform.

The Ensemble for Shehnai Performance

The Shehnai is a physically demanding breath-driven instrument (more demanding than the Bansuri), which cannot be performed by a soloist, accompanied only by a percussionist. The ensemble for a Shehnai performance consists of at least three, preferably four, musicians. A three-member group will feature the lead Shehnai player, a Sur Shehnai (drone) player who merely fills the silences, and a percussionist playing the Tasha (kettledrums). A four-member troupe will feature an additional lead Shehnai player, who can provide intermittent relief to the main musician. In recent times, the Tasha has often been replaced by the Tabla. But, this has not radically altered the fact that hosting a Shehnai concert is more expensive than hosting, for instance, a Sitar or Sarod concert. And, if travel costs get added to the event, the economics become daunting.

The Fading Shehnai

In the pre-Independence era, feudal and ecclesiastical patronage had created a substantial base of Shehnai musicianship. Once the electronic media could take its music to every home, this reservoir threw up the phenomenon called Bismillah Khan. In response to my query, Suresh Chandvankar, an expert on the recording industry, identified eight Shehnai players, whose 78 rpm recordings were published between 1920 and 1947. He also reports that most of the repertoire on these discs is serious art music — ragas in Khayal format, rather than folk or semi-classical genres.

For a recording industry in its infancy, and in an era dominated overwhelmingly by vocal music, this should be considered impressive. Eight Shehnai players recorded commercially between 1920 and 1947 could well outnumber the count logged between 1947 and 2007. After Independence, there has been a steady decline in the number of Shehnai artists on the concert platform. As a result, today a credible Shehnai player below the age of 50 is almost impossible to find.

What Explains the Impending Famine

The full-time employment of Shehnai players is now history. The first blow came when democratic India disbanded the princely states. Gradually thereafter, the wealthy temples, once significant employers of Shehnai players, discontinued the practice. The radio network never considered the Shehnai worthy of protectionist intervention. Like all other musicians, the Shehnai player was thus progressively exposed to market forces.

The clue to the Shehnai's plight lies in the changing tastes of its bread-and-butter market. Electronic synthesisers and brass bands are fast taking over the ceremonial and religious market. Marriages on the silver screen, which were once sanctified by Shehnai music, are following suit. The Shehnai is still heard — even if occasionally — in the religious and ceremonial context. But, in most cases, you are hearing a Bismillah Khan recording, rather than a live performance, or a recording of a lesser known Shehnai artist.

Nothing is taking the place of traditional sources of livelihood to attract new talent to the Shehnai art. There is no incentive for an aspirant to undergo 10/15 years of training in art music, and then market the high-cost services of a three or four-men troupe to a lukewarm market. The cultivation of a foreign market might have created a supplementary avenue. But, this opportunity suffered from neglect as Bismillah Khan, the only exponent with an international following, was a reluctant traveller.

Ali Ahmed Hussain

The cultural process is constantly pulling some instruments upwards, and pushing others downwards, in terms of popularity and stature. The logic of this process is inscrutable. The Shehnai, however, may warrant a different perspective.

Bismillah Khan emerged from a musical culture well endowed with Shehnai musicianship, but left behind a famine. The virtual evaporation of talent from an instrument within two generations is difficult to explain. This may well be because it is not musicianship that failed the Shehnai after Bismillah, but the Shehnai that failed musicianship. Possibly, the instrument itself required a re-think in the current context.

Rethinking the Shehnai

Two issues may be considered, with the caveat that they are merely speculations. One pertains to the acoustic properties of the instrument, while the other pertains to the format and idiom of the music.

The Shehnai was designed as an outdoor instrument. Its shrill, piercing sound was designed for travelling long distances without amplification and collecting people at the commencement of ceremonies, and not necessarily for the pleasantness of its aural experience. The pair of kettledrums accompanying the Shehnai was, likewise, designed for loudness rather than sweetness.

The Shehnai and the accompanying drums were designed in the pre-amplification era. Once modern electronics appeared on the scene, and the relationship with the audiences changed, the pleasantness of its sound could have become a necessity it could not fulfil. Theoretically at least, the Shehnai — like several other instruments — could have been acoustically re-engineered for a microphone-friendly delivery of music.

The second issue could be the raga presentation protocol. The Shehnai renders a raga in the Khayal format. But, the music-scape has changed dramatically in the last quarter of the twentieth century. Contemporary audiences may not relate to the Khayal format on the Shehnai as comfortably as they once did. Today's audiences might have acquired a bias favouring instrumental music which is noticeably different from vocal music in the totality of the musical experience. This possibility is suggested by the success with which the Bansuri and Sarangi — both under the Khayal influence till recently — have drifted towards non-Khayal stylistics in recent times.

Theoretically, therefore, a genius, who rethinks and reinvents the Shehnai in all important respects, may yet restore it to the art music platform. Considering the miniscule base of musicianship left, the prospects are not encouraging. This is lamentable also in its broader context, because the Shehnai shares its impending extinction with the Sarangi and the Rudra Veena — two other instruments of entirely Indian origin.

20

The Pakhawaj and Tabla
Everybody Wants Zakir

E very musician in India wants Zakir to accompany him. Every assembly of Indian connoisseurs wants to hear a Zakir solo. Every Kathak dancer wants Zakir to add sizzle to her footwork. Every world music ensemble wants Zakir as the lead percussionist. And, every student of the Tabla wants to be a Zakir. This is, undoubtedly, the triumph of a charismatic genius called Zakir Hussain. But, it is also the victory of the Indian art of percussion, and of rhythm as a musical expression sufficient unto itself.

Zakir Hussain is a product of the north Indian art music tradition of transforming geocentric time into musical time, which began with the Pakhawaj several millennia ago, and continues with the Tabla.

Pakhawaj

The Pakhawaj (originally known as Mridang) is a venerated instrument. The Mridangam of Carnatic music belongs to the same family. Mythology attributes the Mridang's origination to Brahma, the Creator of the universe. Such notions often suggest indeterminate antiquity and untraceable origins.

Raja Chhatrapati Singh

Up to eighteenth century, the Mridang/Pakhawaj was the dominant rhythmic accompaniment for art music and even Kathak dance. Today, its presence is largely limited to the Dhrupad genre. The Hindustani mainstream now prefers the Tabla across all modern genres of music. The Pakhawaj, no doubt, still enjoys immense prestige as the originator, developer, and preserver of the rhythmic science and percussion art.

The most widely cited derivation of its name is from Sanskrit: Paksha = side + Vadya = instrument. The Pakhawaj is a horizontal wooden barrel-drum, asymmetrical on one side. Its forearm-powered open-palm playing technique gives its sound a booming resonance and sonorous dignity. In addition to accompaniment, the Pakhawaj also has a solo tradition for connoisseurs of rhythm.

Having been a resident of the Vaishnava temples along with Dhrupad, the Pakhawaj cultivated its art most assiduously in the Mathura/Vrindavan region. From there, it travelled to the Mughal court with Dhrupad, and continued its forward march. The landmark figure in Pakhawaj history was Lala Bhagwandas, a product of the Mathura/Vrindavan tradition, and an esteemed musician at Akbar's court (sixteenth century). His disciples spearheaded Pakhawaj traditions in several parts of the country — Punjab, Uttar Pradesh, Maharashtra, Madhya Pradesh, Gujarat, Rajasthan, and Bengal.

When Dhrupad was declared a "museum piece" in the early years after Independence, this description did not apply to the Pakhawaj because, even at that stage, it claimed a substantial resource of quality musicianship. After European and US markets warmed up to Dhrupad, starting from the 1960s, and gathering steam in the 1980s, the Pakhawaj scene also got a shot of adrenalin. The instrument now shares the fruits of the Dhrupad revival.

The Pakhawaj now appears to be on the threshold of a new market — the global market for Indian and cross-cultural ensembles. Several Hindustani and Carnatic percussion instruments have entered this segment since the 1980s. The entry of the Pakhawaj, though late, is hardly surprising. Any instrument which speaks the language of rhythm with such grace and authority had to, one day, find a global audience.

To this day, the world of the Pakhawaj continues to be more vibrant than either Dhrupad vocalism or the Rudra Veena. On request, Uday Bhawalkar, the Dhrupad vocalist, and Akhilesh Gundecha, the Pakhawaj exponent, compiled for me a list over 20 contemporary Pakhawaj players of concert quality. Aneesh Pradhan, a percussionist and music historian, suspects that many of these 20 could be better soloists than accompanists. Good accompanists, he fears, might still be too few. He attributes the comfortable supply of Pakhawaj players to the additional talent available outside art music — in the devotional music traditions, where the instrument is well entrenched and relatively insulated from market forces.

Tabla

The origin of the Tabla, the vertical drum pair, is a puzzle that defies solution. Its name has a Persian ring to it; but this is not considered evidence of its origin. The instrument came into prominence during the fifteenth century at the dawn of the modern era in Hindustani music. The era began when the Khayal started challenging the supremacy of Dhrupad. In later years, lighter vocal genres like the Thumree and Tappa also became immensely popular. The ponderous Rudra Veena yielded its pre-eminence to the sprightly Sitar. Hindustani music now needed a percussion partner of greater agility, delicate playing technique, and softer output. The Tabla, already a mature instrument by then, steadily enlarged its role on the emerging music-scape, to finally replace the Pakhawaj by the eighteenth century.

Historic developments in the Tabla idiom took place during the reign of Emperor Muhammad Shah of Delhi (1719-48), whose court was also host to the launch of the Sitar, and the maturation of Khayal vocalism. The musician responsible for the percussion revolution was Siddhar Khan Dhadhi.

Siddhar Khan was an accomplished Pakhawaj player, who translated the forearm-powered open-palm Pakhawaj idiom into the wrist-and-fingers idiom of the Tabla, thus creating an entirely new percussion language. His students spread to other major centres of music, and adapted the style to respond to local influences and aesthetic values. As a result, the world of the Tabla now recognises six major styles, known by the names of the centres where they evolved.

(a) Delhi: In recent times, Inam Ali Khan and Lateef Ahmed Khan have been the most distinguished exponents of this gharana.

(b) Ajrada: Habibuddin Khan was the most distinguished percussionist of this style in recent memory.

(c)   Lucknow: Afaque Hussain Khan was the most recent distinguished percussionist of this lineage.

(d)   Farrukhabad: This tradition produced three luminaries in the same generation: Ahmed Jan Thirakwa, Shamsuddin Khan, and Ameer Hussain Khan.

(e)   Benares: This pedigree again produced three outstanding percussionists in the same generation — Shamta Prasad, Kishen Maharaj, and Anokhey Lal.

(f)   Punjab: This style produced the superstars of late twentieth-century music — Allahrakha Khan, and his son, Zakir Hussain. Though masters of their own traditional idiom, the Punjab lineage maestros have enriched it with ideas from several other sources.

Zakir Hussain

The stylistic distinctions between these lineages are, obviously, not as evident in accompaniment, as they are in solo performance, because an accompanist needs to respond spontaneously, free from gharana preferences.

The Tabla as Accompanist and Soloist

Percussion accompaniment for contemporary Hindustani music can be categorised into three levels of presence — supportive, interactive, and competitive.

In accompanying vocalists, whose art is melody-dominant, the Tabla's presence is primarily supportive, though it may become mildly interactive in the brisk movements, and the light and semi-classical genres. With the wind and bow instruments, the percussionist's role is similar because these instruments, by and large, follow the vocal idiom.

The equation changes substantially in the case of string instruments like the Sitar, Sarod, and Santoor. These instruments are either plucked or struck. In the process of activating the sound, they create a rhythmic pattern. This gives the Tabla an opening for an interactive and even competitive relationship with the instrumental idiom.

In order to exploit this potential, instrumentalists have steadily heightened the rhythmic complexity of music, and encouraged percussionists to match it with stroke-craft improvisations. As a result, the collaborative musical effort has become far more engaging, and enlarged the audiences for instrumental music. Progressively, as the string instruments strengthened their hold over the concert platform, they enabled the Tabla to enhance its visibility. This trend also permitted Tabla players to acquire an independent following.

The true test of a percussionist's following is the Tabla solo — a comprehensive and systematic display of mastery over different levels of stroke-density and rhythmic complexity. In the absence of truly towering percussionists, the last quarter of the twentieth century saw a sharp decline in the audiences for Tabla solos. Thanks to today's enhanced visibility for percussion, the solo is now making a comeback, and drawing young listeners. Sadanand Naimpalli, a respected percussion Guru, describes this as "The Zakir Effect".

In terms of aesthetic cultivation, today's audiences for Tabla solos cannot, obviously, be compared to mid-twentieth century audiences. But, the phenomenon does signify a revival of interest in the percussion art, independently of its role as an accompanist. Maybe, it was Zakir Hussain who made it a "happening". But, it is not restricted to Zakir alone. So, the happening was possibly waiting to happen anyway.

The Tabla today commands the largest base of professional, amateur, and aspiring musicianship amongst all Indian instruments. The profession is amply endowed with scholarly as well as creative faculties. The idiom of the instrument is being constantly enriched by contemporary maestros. As an accompanist, soloist or ensemble performer, and in India or abroad, the Tabla is in good health.

21

Harmonium
Controversial, Yet Firmly Entrenched

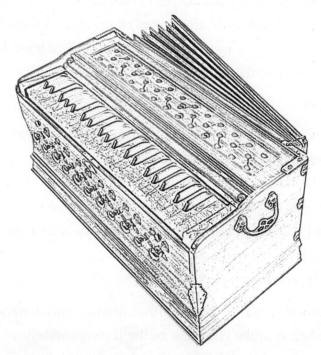

agore called it the "bane of Indian music". The All India Radio banned it for several decades. After a brief involvement, Carnatic music rejected the instrument. In Hindustani music, the Dhrupad genre ignores it. Serious Khayal vocalists express grave reservations about its suitability to art music. When pushed, every professional Harmonium player turns defensive about his instrument. Attempts to establish it as a solo instrument have failed. Despite the ongoing debate over its musical value, the Harmonium holds sway over vocal accompaniment not only in Hindustani art music, but in all musical genres of northern India. It could be the most widely owned and heard instrument in the country, and claim an enormous base of amateur and professional musicianship.

The Harmonium began replacing the Sarangi towards the end of the nineteenth century, and now appears firmly entrenched. The instrument mechanised the acoustically standardised execution of notes, which Sarangi or Violin players achieve only after years of practice. Satisfactory melodic execution came within easier reach of an unprecedented number of musicians. This became the driving force of the instrument's popularity.

The Instrument

The Harmonium belongs to a family of keyboard based wind instruments which includes a variety of organs, and various types of accordions. The design of the Harmonium was patented by a Frenchman, Alexander Dubain in 1840. His design, as it came to India, had the keyboard and reed-panel mounted on a pedestal, primed by foot-pedals for activating the bellows. The instrument was originally played much like a piano with all ten fingers, and with the player sitting on a chair.

The instrument came to India with Christian missionaries, and was probably first heard in the churches of the three presidencies — Calcutta, Bombay and Madras (now Kolkata, Mumbai and Chennai respectively). It entered Indian music in the 1880s through the regional theatre, where it became a sensation. Interestingly, the Marathi Theatre continued to call it an "organ" much as the churches did. Its main advantage was the volume of the output, richness of its sound and — unlike the string instruments — the convenience of not requiring retuning during a performance. In the theatre of the pre-amplification era, the Harmonium probably also enabled the engagement of a smaller orchestra, thus bringing down costs.

The precise timing of the Harmonium's entry into art music is not known. The direction was, however, to be expected because of its practical advantages (see chapter on the Sarangi). It also helped that the regional theatre had, by then, nurtured a substantial base of competent players with a reasonable foundation of raga grammar. Outside the theatre, however, the instrument faced an initial hurdle.

The concert platform was not willing to accept an instrument whose player sat on a chair — a level above the vocalist. The problem was solved around 1890 in consultation with the patent-holders and Indian musicians. The result was a compact and portable Harmonium with its bellows mounted at the rear. The Harmonium player could now sit on the floor, and pump the bellows with one hand, while the other hand executed the melody. With this change, the vocalist could also choose to accompany himself/herself.

After this modification, the instrument took north Indian music by storm. By 1910, the Harmonium had reached the remotest corner of India and entered all segments of north Indian music — folk, devotional, semi-classical, and popular. By then, it was also easing the Sarangi off the stage in art music. When imports from Europe were disrupted during the Second World War, booming domestic demand gave birth to a sizeable base of Indian suppliers. Prices tumbled and sales soared.

Landmark Personalities

The Harmonium wave was stimulated in Bengal and Maharashtra by the stature of a few iconic personalities. Their profiles demonstrate the instrument's early linkages with the worlds of theatre and semi-classical music.

The instrument became a contender for the art music space with Bhaiyya Ganpatrao (1852-1923), a member of princely establishment of Gwalior, who lived mostly in Calcutta. He was trained in Dhrupad, Khayal, and the Rudra

Bhaiya Ganpatrao

Veena, but fell in love with the Thumree genre, and the newly arrived Harmonium. He became a formidable Harmonium player, and also groomed some of the most outstanding Thumree singers of the era. In the next generation, the Harmonium received a huge impetus in Maharashtra through the person of Govindrao Tembe (1881-1955). Tembe was a brilliant self-taught Harmonium player, and a vocalist trained by the redoubtable Bhaskarbuwa Bakhle (1869-1922). Tembe was actively involved in Marathi Theatre as a composer, and is credited with memorable compositions, especially in Thumree style. Tembe also emerged later as a respected man of letters.

From the middle of the twentieth century, the Harmonium's stature was boosted by Gyan Prakash Ghosh in Bengal, and P.L. Deshpande in Maharashtra.

Ghosh was a versatile genius — Tabla exponent, Harmonium player, and composer. The list of his students, covering all segments of musical activity, reads like a Who's Who of music in Bengal. He reportedly supervised the design developments undertaken by Dwarka & Sons, a leading Harmonium manufacturer in Calcutta. P.L. Deshpande in Maharashtra was, likewise, much larger than the Harmonium he played with distinction. He was a towering literary personality, also highly respected in theatre circles.

In subsequent generations, Bengal and Maharashtra — the most prolific nurseries of musical talent — have continued to produce outstanding Harmonium exponents, as well as eminent vocalists who excelled as Harmonium players.

The Harmonium and Art Music

Semi-classical and light music — the Ghazal and the Thumree — admitted the Harmonium before art music did. This happened perhaps because the instrument was adequate for the requirements of these poetry-dominant genres while also being very practical. The issue became tricky in the context of a raga-bound and melody-dominant genre like the Khayal.

The Harmonium is widely acknowledged as being unsuitable for

Govindrao Tembe

accompanying Hindustani vocal music. Its critics point towards two facets of its design. The basic problem lies with the 12 fixed notes within each octave. To do justice to Hindustani music, an instrument needs to deliver 22 notes, including fractional notes. The secondary problem lies in the keyboard-based design. A keyboard instrument cannot faithfully execute every kind of intervallic transition that is used in Hindustani vocalism. When compared to bowed alternatives like the Sarangi and the Violin, it falls short on musical value.

The proponents of the Harmonium argue that both these problems are exaggerated. They insist that, with astute control over the pumping and fingering, a competent player can deliver all the melodic nuances of Hindustani vocalism. They contend that an expert player can even create an illusion of the fractional notes which are missing from the instrument's acoustic design.

As an ambitious response to the challenge of fractional notes, innovators have now developed a "Shruti (Microtone) Harmonium", which can explicitly execute 22 notes. This innovation has yet to register its presence on the concert platform.

Why the Harmonium Reigns

Considering that its musical value remains controversial a century after its adoption, we need to explain the Harmonium's monopolistic position.

Gyan Prakash Ghosh

The foremost factor is economics. The Harmonium has spawned such a large resource of musicianship that either alternative — Sarangi or Violin — would be several times more expensive to hire. The second factor arises partially from the first. A huge base of musicianship inevitably throws up a few outstanding musicians, whose engagement rates may be higher, but are not prohibitive. And, indeed, the Harmonium has produced several such musicians, primarily in Maharashtra and Bengal. They have become preferred accompanists to the leading vocalists, and also attracted exceptional talent as students.

When a quality service is available at a sensible price, the system will tend to resist change — until the consumer revolts. Audiences — as a class — seem to be in no mood to revolt, even if a small minority is dissatisfied. A broadly similar situation prevails amongst vocalists. Serious vocalists continue to lament the demise of the Sarangi, and the compromised musical values of the Harmonium. And, yet, they live with it because, though not entirely acceptable, the Harmonium is not insufferable.

To be fair, some leading vocalists of earlier generations are known to have preferred the Harmonium to the Sarangi precisely because it cannot match the vocalist's melodic sophistication. Some eminent vocalists of the past have even refused first-rate Sarangi accompaniment when it was available because they saw it as distracting, intrusive or competitive. Such attitudes are no longer encountered in the musical culture. Today's vocalists work with the Harmonium in a spirit of realism.

P.L. Deshpande

The semi-classical, popular, devotional, and partially even folk music professionals are, in fact, plunging deeper into keyboard territory, with electronic organs accompanying them. The Khayal platform has, however, accepted only the electronic Tanpura so far — that too as an adjunct to an acoustic Tanpura. For the present, therefore, art music appears to be a safe haven for the Harmonium.

The only stress-point in this situation is that Harmonium players are paid poorly in relation to their musicianship. Increasingly, trained exponents of the instrument are pursuing other professions, and treating the art music stage as a hobby. Fewer young musicians are training to become Harmonium players. A part of the trained talent is mastering electronic keyboards, and drifting towards the popular music industry. Over the next few decades, therefore, Harmonium accompanists for art music could become less plentiful, and need to be paid much better. It is difficult to predict how the major players in the business will respond to such a situation.

Implications for Hindustani Vocalism

The Harmonium culture has struck deep roots in non-peninsular India. It is normal for students of vocal music to be first taught to play the Harmonium, and then to sing to its accompaniment in order to achieve pitch perfection. This dependence on the Harmonium lasts several years, till the student is ready to sing accompanied by the Tanpura.

During these years, three things have most likely happened. Firstly, the singer's intonation has been perfected for 12 notes, and not for all the 22 required of a complete art music performer. Secondly, the singer's vocalisation organs and melodic imagination have been programmed to function with only 12 notes. As a result, ragas that require intonation beyond the 12 notes of a Harmonium either tend to get neglected, or are rendered clumsily. Thirdly, the vocalist's treatment of melody has begun to reflect the Harmonium's limitations in sculpting and ornamentation. These infirmities acquired in the most formative years are not easily reversed later because the concert platform imposes the Harmonium on the vocalist once again — now as an accompanist.

A few of today's vocalists have, indeed, risen above the aesthetic indoctrination inherent in the Harmonium culture, and achieved eminence as musicians. The instrument cannot, therefore, be held wholly responsible for the widespread depletion of melodic subtleties observed in Khayal vocalism. However, having dominated Hindustani vocalism for three or four generations, could the Harmonium have contributed to this loss by legitimising melodically handicapped music?

Suggested Readings

Musical Aesthetics

Green, Barry. The Mastery of Music. 2003. Oxford, Pan Macmillan

Hanslick, Eduard. 1974, The beautiful in Music, London, New York, Novello, Ewer & Co.

Mathieu, WA. 1994. The Musical Life. Boston. Shambhala Books.

McLeish, Kenneth (Ed.) 1993. Key Ideas in Human Thought: New York. Facts on File Inc.

Rao, Suvarnalata, 2000, Acoustical Perspectives on Raga-Rasa Theory, Delhi, Munshiram Manoharlal

Saxena, Susheel Kumar, 2009. Hindustani Music and Aesthetics Today. New Delhi, Sangeet Natak Akademi.

Seashore, Carl, 1967, Psychology of Music. Mineola, NY, Dover Publications

General: Hindustani Music

Bhatkhande, Vishnu Narayan (Hindi). Bhatkhande Sangeet Shastra, vol. I to IV. Hathras, Sangeet Karyalaya.

Garg, Lakshmi Narayan (ed.). 1989. (Hindi). Nibandha Sangeet, Hathras, Sangeet Karyalaya.

Jaidev Singh, Thakur, 1995, Indian Music, Calcutta: Sangeet Research Academy.

Mishra, Susheela. 2001. Among Contemporary Musicians, New Delhi, Harman Publishing House.

Mehta, Ramanlal (ed.) 1993. Composition in Hindustani Music. Baroda, Indian Musicological Society.

Prajnananand, Swami, 1973, Historical Development of Indian Music. Calcutta, Firma KL Mukhopadhyaya.

Raja, Deepak S. 2005. Hindustani Music — A tradition in transition. New Delhi, DK Printworld.

Ranade, Ashok D. 1984, On the Music and Musicians of Hindoostan. Delhi, Promilla & Co.

Ranade, Ashok D, 1993. Hindustani Music. Delhi. National Book Trust of India.

The Hindu Speaks on Music, 1999. Chennai, Kasturi & Sons.

Genres of Music

Deshpande, Vamanrao H, 1973, Indian Musical Traditions — An aesthetic study of Gharanas in Hindustani Music. Bombay, Popular Prakashan.

Deshpande, Vamanrao H, 1989, Between Two Tanpuras. Bombay, Popular Prakashan.

Deodhar, BR. 1993. Pillars of Hindustani Music, Bombay, Popular Prakashan.

Manuel, Peter, 1989. Thumri in Historical and Stylistic Perspectives, Delhi, Motilal Banarasidass.

Nadkarni, Mohan, 1999, The Great Masters — Profiles in Hindustani Classical Vocal Music, Delhi, Harper Collins.

Raja, Deepak S., and Rao, Suvarnalata (ed.). 1999. Perspectives on Dhrupad, Baroda, Indian Musicological Society.

Raja, Deepak S. 2009, Khayal Vocalism — Continuity within Change, New Delhi. DK Printworld.

Shrivastava, Indurama, 1980. Dhrupada — A Study of Its Origin, Historical Development, Structure and Present State. Delhi. Motilal Banarasidass.

Shukla, Shatrughna 1983 (Hindi). Thumri ki Utpatti, Vikas aur Saheliyan. Delhi, University of Delhi.

Wade, Bonnie C. 1984, Khyal: Creativity within North India's Classical Music Tradition. London, New York, Cambridge University Press.

Organology and Instrumental Music

Bor, Joep, 1987, The Voice of the Sarangi, Bombay, Journal of the National Centre for the Performing Arts.

Deva, BC. 1977. Indian Musical Instruments, Delhi. National Book Trust of India.

Kasliwal, Suneera, 2001. Classical Musical Instruments. New Delhi, Rupa & Co.

Miner, Allyn, 1997. Sitar and Sarod in the 18th and 19th Centuries. Delhi, Motilal Banarasidass.

Sangeet Research Academy, 1990. Calcutta/ Mumbai: Proceedings of the Seminar on the Sitar.

Sangeet Research Academy, 1991. Calcutta/ Mumbai: Proceedings of the Seminar on the Sarod.

Sangeet Research Academy, 1993. Calcutta/ Mumbai: Proceedings of the Seminar on Instrument Makers. .

Sangeet Research Academy, 1997. Calcutta/ Mumbai: Proceedings of the Seminar on the Tanpura.

Index